SCENES FROM A LONG SLEEP

Peter Didsbury was born in 1946 in Fleetwood, Lancashire. He moved to Hull at the age of six, and read English and Hebrew at Oxford. After teaching English in Hull for eight years, he turned to the past for employment as well as for inspiration, becoming an archaeologist. The first edition of his retrospective *Scenes from a Long Sleep: New & Collected Poems* (Bloodaxe Books, 2003) drew on three previous Bloodaxe collections, *The Butchers of Hull* (1982), *The Classical Farm* (1987) and *That Old-Time Religion* (1994), plus a new collection, *A Natural History*. An expanded edition – also drawing upon a later collection, *A Fire Shared* (2020), along with new and previously uncollected poems – was published by Bloodaxe Books in 2026 to mark his 80th birthday. He won a Cholmondeley Award for *The Classical Farm*, which was a Poetry Book Society Recommendation, as was *That Old-Time Religion*.

PETER DIDSBURY

SCENES FROM A LONG SLEEP

NEW & COLLECTED POEMS

EXPANDED EDITION

BLOODAXE BOOKS

ISBN: 978 1 78037 822 0

This edition first published 2026 by
Bloodaxe Books Ltd,
Eastburn,
South Park,
Hexham,
Northumberland NE46 1BS.

Expanded from the original edition published in 2003.

www.bloodaxebooks.com
For further information about Bloodaxe titles
please visit our website and join our mailing list
or write to the above address for a catalogue.

Supported using public funding by
ARTS COUNCIL
ENGLAND

Printed by Lightning Source at the printing works identified by the code inside the back cover.

For David Edgar, Annie, Robert and Louise

CONTENTS

The Classical Farm (1987)

The Butchers of Hull (1982)

ACKNOWLEDGEMENTS

The original 2003 edition of this book included all the poems from Peter Didsbury's previous three Bloodaxe collections *The Butchers of Hull* (1982), *The Classical Farm* (1987) and *That Old-Time Religion* (1994), together with a new collection, *A Natural History* (2003). This expanded edition of *Scenes from a Long Sleep: New & Collected Poems* also includes all the poems from *A Fire Shared*, published by LegalHighsPress in Hull in 2020 with photographs by Ken Steedman, as well as the previously uncollected later poems in the *Post Hoc* (2026) section, all first published here apart from 'A letter never sent, in 1983, to one who had moved away' which appeared in *14 magazine*.

POST HOC

(2026)

I have made a heap of all that I could find

NENNIUS

Blue plaque

One of his high windows
was open as I passed,
allowing in
the autumn afternoon

A little later,
coming back that way
I saw it had been closed
and began to imagine
the ways in which
I might have witnessed this

ways that should command
though purely fictive
a level of compassion
to which I would need to aspire

not least for having seen
as it reached out into the light
a long arm, perhaps,
or heard the dull sound
of something being pulled shut
among the glistening trees

A letter never sent, in 1983, to one who had moved away

A fox on the strand, but nobody believed you.
I share your indignation and surprise.

I use the word *strand* instead of *beach*,
as somehow seeming more appropriate
to the Viking whale-hook of Spurn,
which is where you tell me it happened.

I spell this out in case by any mischance
those fools who can't imagine a fox eating crabs,
preferring to disbelieve whatever they're told,
have suddenly been licensed to read our mail.
I would hate to make their work more difficult.

We had a baby daughter three months ago tonight.
I would have let you know about it sooner
but I've foolishly been trying to write her poems.

Fractured haiku

My hand out of fo/cus,
my breath disturbing
the/surface of the drink

A Christmas poem for 1971

Out of the North there sails a swan.
The length of half the world's high waters,
towards Bethlehem.

For a month of nights beneath the moon
she paddles with a cold intent. Noiselessly,
and quite alone.

The cruel wind does not disturb her vacancy,
neither do the waves.
And when she plunges deep to feed
she feels no pity for what she feeds on.
How could she? It is not in her nature.

But look. She passes with her wings behind her
curved like a bowl of sweet night air
for now she is a bride advancing,
though does not know it, for knowledge
is not required of her.

And neither are the more familiar shepherds,
magi, kings, tyrant
at all conscious of her presence,
a week out from Cyprus, beneath the firmament.

The solitary, clear-flung note she utters, though,
declares she has sailed from far beyond Christmas
towards her Lord of Christmas,
clad in all accustomed whiteness as her greeting.

Now, instinct fulfilled, she circles once and turns to go.
Still unaware, but patterning all things by that meeting
back through Biscay, with its gales and snow.

In for a penny

Not sure where
you'd go to get
green arsenic these days

Or why,
having got some,
you would choose to smear it
across an egg-white cloth

Can't see much point
in crushing strawberries, either,
(unless you just wanted
to make a bigger mess?)

Give you joy

A ladder, a wall
and just enough sunlight to
tell the time by were

all that was needed
to bring into being this
haikumometer

(round and round the sun
go a paint-spattered wall, some
white chrysanthemums)

In the eighties

The bricks had gone back in the oven.
The sun was pouring out
its contents from a jug.
Familiar patterns
of old vendetta and earthquake
had cracked the brown lawns.
The poet sat expiring in the shade.
Whatever in those days
was occupying his thoughts
(we spoke Fahrenheit then)
is mostly now forgotten.
Some tiny blue flowers of thyme by the path, perhaps,
but not much else besides.
He'd have liked, I think I recall,
to learn yet one more language, but which?
He makes up a word for *farm*,
and scratches it with its imagined glyph in the dust.
His poem about Memory
will feature the camel
he once thought he saw
in a film of one of Shakespeare's history plays,
an interloper in a muddy English field.
He tries to engage
with a total recall of the cool
but then gasps, as if at *seraphim*.
Turbaned scholars
(we spoke Fahrenheit then)
are kneeling to inspect
the earth of his garden for texts.

Autumn crocuses

(after Guillaume Apollinaire)

The field is poisonous but pretty in the autumn
The cows that graze there
Are slowly poisoned
The meadow saffron colour of eye shadows lilac
Flowers there your eyes are like that flower
Mauve like their lids and like this autumn
My life which for your eyes' lack
                                        is pure poison

The kids come with emotion
Dressed in smocks and playing the mouth organ
They pick *les colchiques* which are like their mothers
Their daughters' daughters and are your eyelids' colour
Blinking like these flowers blink
                                        in the mad wind

The cow herd sings softly
Behind him moving moaning his cows abandon
For ever this large meadow the ill-
                                        flowered autumn

Allowable language

Autumn afternoon.
Curled and dessicated leaves
get skimmed by the wind
across the gunmetal pond.
I resist their urgent invitation
to address them as 'frail craft',
then make my way home,
only to find
(albeit a whole year later)
that their 'coracle cargoes'
of air have become these words.

A short account of the Russian Empire

(FROM *The Universal Museum and Complete Magazine of Knowledge and Pleasure*, JULY 1769)

Emperor and sole sovereign of all the Russias
whose revenues are variously computed
sovereign lord of Moscow
revenues arising sovereign lord
of Kiow Wlodimiria and Novogrod
from the demesne lands
occupied by peasants Czar in Casan
3 hundred and 50 thousand
each one paying
an hundred and 10 copeiks a year
Czar in Astracan and Siberia
amounting in all to 3 hundred
and 96 thousand roubles
and from the inns and drinking houses
lord of Pleskow
which are about 2 millions
the privilege of selling
beer mead and malt spirit
monopolised by the crown
great duke of Smolensko
and from the tolls and customs
by land and sea duke of
Livonia and Carelia
from the trade carried on by the crown
in iron ptash and ashes of the willow tree
duke of Tweria
and rhubarb tar and train oil
lord of Ingria
and from the salt works
duke of Pernia and Wiataka and Bulgaria
which yearly bring into the treasury
seven hundred thousand roubles

the duty on stampt paper
lord of several other territories
amounting to one hundred
and 20 thousand roubles
great duke of Novogrod
a tax on law suits 10 per cent
of the value contested
duke in the low country
of Tshernikow
from hearth money and bath stoves
in Resan Rostow and Iaroslaw
and from all the hackney horses and carriages
and in Bielosero
the abbey lands managed by a special commission
and in Uldoria
for the benefit of the crown
set as thick as possible with diamonds
his royal standard yellow
duke of Obdoria and Condinia
men of war at Revel and Cronstadt
twenty-four ships of the line
and the galley fleet at St Petersburgh
the caravans to China duke of Esthonia
which is never less
than a hundred thousand roubles
consisting of one hundred and 2 gallies
emperor of all the northern parts
and the produce of the publics shows
of tumblers and rope dancers
lord of the territory of Juweria
of which multitudes are exhibited at Easter
for the diversion of the people
who are passionately fond of them
lord of the Carthalinian czars
allotted for paying
the expenses of the police

and paving the streets
to administer justice
and protect and maintain
the true Greek religion
lord of the Grewzinizn and Georgecan czars
besides this every householder paying
an assessment of his house and courtyard
lord of the Cabardinian princes
an hundred and 50 tables spread
twice a day at the Russian court
a title accorded by all of Europe
and served with 18 hundred dishes
lord and supreme ruler
of many other countries and territories
for which purpose the Court Purveyor receives
2 thousand roubles every 3 days
exclusive of the produce of the crown estates
his robe of purple satin lined with sable
each of whom pays an hundred
and 10 copeiks a year
and the proper quantities of wine sugar and spices
amounting in all to
3 hundred and 96 thousand roubles
the daily consumption of coffee amounting to
one pud or 36 pounds weight
his royal standard yellow
sufficient to maintain
twenty-four ships of the line seven frigates
three bomb ketches and two flat boats
make subject to his will all barbarous nations
and within it the arms of Russia
and seven thousand puds of salt
are expended monthly
and the inhabitants of Siberia
pay most of their tribute in furs

A FIRE SHARED

(2020)

One of them who was blind smiled as he watched the falling snow

ORHAN PAMUK

Chan eil an duslach lag
(The dust is not weak)

SOMAHIRLE MACGILL-EAIN (SORLEY MACLEAN)

The Fog

The fog makes it sound
as if lightweight bones
are falling from the trees,
among which I notice,
as if I hold myself responsible,
the fern-like mountain ash
at the end of my neighbour's yard,
seeded by a passing bird
a handful of years
before I came to live here,
maybe even earlier.
A smoky late October afternoon
in which berries have been eaten
declines in its own slow time
to a midnight as muffled
and seamless as a spell,
from which this very garden door left open,
although by someone else,
now ushers exactly similar vapours
into the house,
or a cat the distant
grandsire of this my guest,
or else, conceivably, no relation at all.

A Fire Shared

This evening I have spent
in the Irishwoman's room.
A fire shared is a fire cheaper.

A twelvemonth since
I knew her not at all.
Our hearths were crowded then
but now it is fitting
that one of them bides cold.
A fire shared is a fire cheaper by far.

She has enough English now
for January tales
of our slavering *bargeist,*
which stalks these dark flagged yards
intent on the taking of children.
She would not have understood a year ago.

A year ago her English was just enough
for blessing or cursing,
to ask the price of bread
or directions to a pump.
But now a fire shared
is a fine instructive tutor.

She has enough English now
to match my *bargeists* and goblins
with *pookas* and suchlike,
and I find I have learned what these are,
from many a night
spent sharing and cheapening fire.

A twelvemonth ago I would not have known
the Irish for 'sorrow', 'cholera', 'children',
or who stood by me at the same wide grave-mouth
as we wept after each of our fashions.
But now I know these things,
which are things I have learned
in the school of the ruined hearth,
which is held in both our rooms,
where a fire shared
is the cheapest fire of all.

Stepping Outside

Mauve and cream crayon colour,
In secluded spots
Throughout the winter garden

As if a passing artist
Had pursued some promising
Line of questioning here

And then gone on his way
Leaving behind as he walked
Just a few sheets torn from his pad

And the crumpled hellebores hanging their heads
In what only a fool
Would dare to mistake for shyness

And which only a fool
Would refuse, even if just for a moment
To identify as such

Braxy-Hams

The hams of those sheep which die of the braxy.

JOHN McTAGGART,
Scottish Gallovidian Encyclopedia, 1824

I am your moorland lover.
I bring you braxy hams.
Slung across my saddle-bow.
To aid my lover's cause.

The sheep it died last autumn.
I found it on the hill.
I shook it thrice, to try its strength,
And it did not fall apart.

Although it died of the braxy, dear,
It's no bad food when ham'd.
The smell in a great measure leaves it, then.
I've had a slice myself.

It's no bad food when ham'd, my queen,
As your mother will not deny.
I've tried a slice or two myself
On my farm behind the hill.

On my farm behind the hill, my dear,
To which I'll carry you soon.
To which you'll go 'cross my saddle-bow,
On top of the braxy-hams.

Lines of Enquiry

(for Sylvie and Olivier Gouchet)

Good job you came from France when you did
to photograph our former Queen and Empress.
As we loom towards each other
through white December
mists this morning
I note she's acquired
an Adolf Hitler moustache.
Overnight, presumably.
The things that go on in this park.
I'd been thinking about
The Blessed Ramon Llull,
and wondering why his canonisation
has been so long delayed,
but now this train of thought has been broken.
A guy comes up to me and says,
he knows it's an odd thing to ask,
but can I tell him what day it is today.
I'm really surprised by his Dorset accent,
so it takes me a while, but Friday,
definitely Friday.

A Closing Prospect

Sudden exhilaration
of late morning sun in the backstreets.
The late winter or early spring as it may be
morning sunlight. My car
corners in the keen air, seemingly with intent,
leaps forward to land on the iron bridge
which spans the muddy drain.
A chain-link fence glints dully on the left,
a hundred yards or so of it holding back
a ragged and half-hearted crowd of thorns,
muffled with torn festoons of carrier bag.
I suddenly see myself
returning by night to stand beneath cold stars,
with kerosene, to walk a cleansing line of flame
along the reflective running parallel waters.
I might simply be imagining
what the summer, given time, will accomplish anyway,
but it doesn't feel like that. It feels like joy,
a joy that has sat down next to me
in the empty passenger seat.
I think I could become quite passionate about hedgerows.
The thought seems to function
as an acceptance of things as they are,
which is not only incomprehensible
but also, perhaps, irrevocable.
When the last corner affords a closing prospect
of my office windows, high in a corner of the old school,
Victorian alms-houses' court and clock-tower next to it,
I even flirt with the idea
that I could come to be reconciled
to having to go through the whole damn thing again,
the whole long shameful business and waste of breath,
if only for the sake of turning slowly

through these gates one more time,
between their brick piers, to park, then sit a while,
then step from my rapidly cooling vehicle
out into such a morning, such an amazement of light.

A Pasture for Gazelles

The solace of standing. Early morning light coming in through the small square window discovers my neighbour's wall to me, the marks of mould and hand and fire on individual bricks, for these are old houses.

Something I wanted to say about walking in the park has become an insight of such lucidity that it's now been absorbed and forgotten.

The dog lies on the lawn, cracking open a peach stone I'm sure I remember tossing onto that flower bed years ago, long before he was born.

The keeper's mower stands quietly in the shade, beneath a tree both exotic and small. The light is that of a certain kind of painting. My grandson would consider this a toy, just the right size for him, so many primary colours.

How Wrong Can You Get?

When I went to bed that night
I expected to dream of a wood,
a light rain anointing
the stones of a ruined chapel.

By breakfast time
I knew this hadn't happened,
and was therefore very churlishly inclined
to be very disappointed.

The feeling lasted
till the middle of the morning,
when a sudden movement recalled my sleeping joy
at the sight of a falcon, magnificently perched.

When lunchtime came, the bird still watching,
I was overwhelmed yet charmed to overhear
a colleague give it out as his opinion
that cherubim were, in all essentials,
but dedicated nature sprites, like dryads.

Which simply isn't true,
though it did serve to demonstrate
that there were more ways than dreaming
of visiting that wood, indeed strengthened my conviction
that air and earth and water, summoned,
had responded, in their own laconic way,
by choosing to remind me about fire.

Eleven a.m.

The gentle and hieratic breathing
of a Pharaoh's head,
cast on the kitchen wall
by these instruments of sunlight
and this pile of washing,
is noted for future reference,
the future perhaps tomorrow,
perhaps in fact a Monday.

Through the open doorway
I find I can see
right down to the end of the garden,
where an unkempt bush
is doing something very similar
with in- and ex-halation,
standing there almost motionless,
in a blue religious haze

Language and Land

1

Towering, turreted,
most complete and entire.
Cross-grained, bad-humoured,
as if through want of tobacco.
Dry, without condiment or kitchen.
Topsy-turvy, without anything other
than meal or potatoes or sky.
Absence of rain, a fit of sickness,
a very large fire, having
smoke but not much flame.
Fair weather for every
willing, skilful man.
A small heap or stack,
for duck and hobbling woman.

2

Come, yellow wife,
And wind the churn,
Wind the darling churn, my wife.
Come, yellow wife,
And wind the churn.
It won't be long
Before the butter comes.

3

When they were upon me
I would see the words running
like tongues of green flame,
along the divots
between thatch and top of wall

When I stood in my doorway
the stretching out

of the long spring evening
would be like the coming home
of pale, imponderable
cattle to the farmstead

Words at Skipsea Brough

The dissenting minister whose destiny it was
to become this blasted elm,
on the bed of this dried-up mere,
leans slightly forward as if from a pulpit,
single branch extended
above what is now his only congregation,
some inattentive cows. Observe him well.
The hair is gone,
and the eyes have failed to remain.
What once was richly garbed in black
is now a leprous white.
He raised his arm to fulminate
just once too often, it seems,
and can only, now, of our charity, be supposed
not to have noticed, or even felt, a thing,
that last of all nights,
any urgency of sky,
or the lightning reversing its flow.

The Conclave

That his mind was strange
was what they had to tell him

That he was well aware of it
was the essence of his reply

At which point the heavens
did what afterwards none could remember

Leaving suddenly none
with the will to pursue the matter

Or that strange-minded person
much further into the forest

The Evening Star

The evening star last night,
Pulsing and burning white
Above the Victorian park,
Harbour of consolation and philosophy.

Or, as turned out to be the case,
The Police helicopter,
Hanging on station a couple of miles away,
Motionless in the currents of the sky.

It did not feel like deception, why should it?
For at other times the planet Herself
Has indeed led me safely home
And once, in similitude of a message,
Climbed to stand directly adjacent
To the crescent moon
On the roof of the Friday mosque.

Sky and earth religions
Have both found their welcome here,
Can sometimes not be distinguished.
Walking these gardens I have lately come to perceive
The firmament as something that observes me,
A scrutinising Face, like those old alchemical suns
But vast, vast, and therefore featureless.
Or I have seen the graceful heft
Of a chestnut's canopy up into the light,
Or a congregation of doves
Come down in the rain on the roof of the keeper's lodge,
Arranging their plump notes
Like breves on the stave of the pantiles,
Waiting to be sung.

As, in fact, are all things,
And sometimes not even in vain.
An elderly person, treading these selfsame paths
In a time when the park was new,
Is suddenly bidden out of nowhere to remember
The excitement of a poem from his youth
And in that moment, as if watching from a tower,
Or from a peak in Darien,
Sheds the wasted years and begins to live for ever,
As long delayed waves from the distant heart of stillness
Break around him on the shores of possibility.

Travellers

A tethered horse
stands grazing among gulls,
on a grassy bank
beside an industrial stream

In a painting hidden in a cupboard somewhere
I'm walking down
a railway embankment towards them
as if stepping out of a history

The cold wind blows
and the cold wind blows

The morning wind
breathes coldly upon
the still-furled leaves
of some ragged hedgerow trees,
and glazes them
with an almost adhesive light

Angelophany

(in memoriam T.F. Griffin)

I glimpsed him as I awoke,
though I cannot believe I was meant to,
head bowed, wings furled,
as he stooped to exit my chamber.

For he'd left such light behind, candescence,
that only when it had suffered enough
to congeal again into matter
did I dare to test my new eyes.

I could learn no way to open
the sealed jar that I found there,
high as a servant. As the afternoon commenced
I concluded that unless I sent out for a stone

and broke it at the shoulder,
which is what I then did, I should never
possess my language. My proper words,
which otherwise would rest denied to me,

must be hurled with violence from their violable home,
like doves from a tower, or birds from a sea-cliff,
to fly into the east above the waves
before wheeling far out and finally turning inland.

He had come while I slept, I suppose,
and had not meant me to see him,
just to discover the jar he would leave there,
then break it, observing its sherds

rock to stillness on the floor,
becoming in terms of that pearl-encrusted room
as dawn light breaking the windows yet again,
or any familiar item of furniture.

Seasonal References

Rooks chase up and down
in the barely clothed branches,
until the lights change

The bird-feeders sway,
this stillest of all mornings,
above the young ferns

In This Street

Under-edge of the cloud mass.
Scraps of dove-grey silk
torn from the lining
of a mid nineteenth-century
minor poet's frock-coat.

Confusion of thought,
as often in this street,
dog dirt and litter-laden gutter
leading down to the river.

Dragging homeward,
that kind of thing,
the sky now suddenly freighted
with forgotten colloquy,
the nacreous conversation
of vanished afternoons.

In a Distant Market

Indignant woman in rubble,
her purse and horsemeat,
wrapped in bloodstained paper,
beside her in the cold.

The shame of it.
to be suddenly so accessible
to the wanton hand of the state.

Trying to raise herself, she becomes aware
of the birds that are starting to land.
In ones and twos at first
but soon from a vortex
the darkly bound rim of which
is proffered like a cup. But by whom?
By peering, aghast, pale faces?
Or by disarrangement of slowly congealing wings?

It doesn't matter. Makes no sense at all.
A priest is saying he'll show her where peacocks lie buried,
an imam throws open a casement to ask the sky
the price of a bag of its silver-plated splinters.

She tries to smile.
How *red* things are. A stew compounded
of pork and brick dust, tomatoes, pepper,
could not be more so. Soon, it seems,
she will live in a house as bright as the fruit of the holly,
sit all day long by its windows, be visited there by the snow.

Ghost Work

An assonance of intercepted voices

1

Hieratic postures,
in and around the house.
In and out of darkening rooms, balletic, jerky,
every kind of
arm and hand movement.
And in the moonlight, too,
in the garden's anointed
timelessness. Do not stop me now.
I am practising being a ghost,
the kind of shade I know I must become.
Or stop me with a glance, should you wish.
But no more words. Not at this late stage.
Why would I want
To have truck with words again?
It is only these actions
Which may help me now to remember
my forgotten future states.
Remember and predict. Predict. Predict them.

2

A ghost threw me down the stairs last night.
He did. Oh yes he did.
It was in the spill from the skylight
As I stood on the silvery landing.

He threw me heavily down and hurt me.
He did. Oh yes he did.
He threw me down the stairs last night
And all because I was singing.

3

There were many secrets,
all of them now forgotten.
Many questions,
none of them ever answered.

It doesn't matter.
In the annals of ghost-work
all that ever gets recorded
is that *walking unseen in daylight*,
at last successfully mastered,
has been irrevocably learned.

4

White smoke hanging a little above the lawn,
like a drape of gauze protecting apple blossom.
Rather strange at midsummer.

Frost on a low outhouse roof
where some cats lie asleep in the sun,
and it isn't even autumn.

Other cats, which were never mine own,
in stately slowness stepping behind each other
down green colonnades,
as if to a musick
of faery lutanists

and now, at last, myself found watching them,
idly watching the garden through them,
in hazy sunlight,
for seconds that seem
to have been turning into years

5

Sometimes I almost think I can remember
birds hanging up outside a poulterer's window,
in a nearby town, naked, necks awry,
inviting themselves to be drawn…

…inviting themselves to be drawn
as if enclosed inside perfect tears,
pendulous, just about to fall
down from downcast eyes,
the downcast eyes
of one seated at this table,
a very long time ago,
down through the centuries
onto this loaf of bread.

6

Ghosts make other ghosts,
Augment their nation,
Don't know why, but they do.

Don't know how they do it,
Or even if they mean to
But do it, you know, they most certainly do do.

Is it by biting, perhaps?
Or by showing of chains
Intended to terrify?
Or is it by some other method?

I've said I don't know, and if I did
I certainly wouldn't tell *you*, or try to explain.
The facts are clear. Ghosts make other ghosts.
Their silent voices, borne behind the wind,
Command our attention,
Will school us both in obedient listening,
Will see us both through eternity, wouldn't you say?

Words at Wharram Percy

26th June 2004

No silence here.
The place is loud with peace.
Blackcap and robin
give voice in the soft June rain,
conspire in their different octaves
with leaf and lawn and stone.
The air retains
millennia of sound. Listen.
An axe-note falls through countless autumns
down the valley's terraced side.
A wife calls out, in Middle English,
to a man who mows in the glebe,
but his blade lisps on as though he has not heard.
Shadow crawls slowly around a mass-dial
scratched on the porch of the church,
dislodging a grain of sand
which falls ringing onto the path.
There is only utterance.
Low-skimming birds pick flies from the tensile
surface of the pond, and each touch rings
as if struck from a vanished bell.
Hillside pasture lies fizzing under the rain,
through which a partridge
hurries her brood to safety
among cowslip, oat grass, Yorkshire fog, black medick.

Bestial Gleanings

The cat's dyslexic.
When he wants out
He must always first go in search
Of his flat cap.

The frog's unlucky.
Out for a stroll
His legs have brought him
To the side door of this fine restaurant.

And then, of course, the crow.
Alone in his high nest
Directly outside my window
He stares towards the river
And caws he can see no ships.

Handshakes

If Søren Kierkegaard had lived to a decent age, instead of dying young, as he did, then he might have visited England, in 1889 or thereabouts, and met Thomas Hardy, or my grandmother. It wouldn't take much imaginative skill to engineer an encounter with another inhabitant of the European cultural milieu, but perhaps all I'd be doing, in that case, would be constructing a simulacrum (for reasons deep and scarcely understood, but not necessarily purposeful) of a recorded meeting between Dickens and that well-known Danish bore Hans Christian Andersen. Bringing him into proximity with my grandmother, who was then a child of twelve, on the other hand, might prove slightly more of a challenge, since it would involve my transporting him to a town in north-west Lancashire, the kind of place where his Danish hat and manners could surely have attracted early and unwelcome attentions. At the moment, I favour his glimpsing her on a summer evening through the half-lowered window of a hansom cab, perhaps drawn up in a sunlit station yard, perhaps as she walked along hand in hand with her father. For her father, of course, given his Scottish origins, I have already managed with no trouble at all to construct a plausible, instructive and amusing chain of handshakes which leads me directly back to Thomas Carlyle.

A Charmed Circle

Chairs left out on the lawn.
Faint but insistent odour of creosote.
No moon. No stars. No us.

Left out 'in the night',
a night when our absence
finds such a home in air
that I don't suppose
it even knows we're here.

It isn't always like this.
There are nights when to sit
imbibing the breath
of the blue geraniums,
the dead white roses,
simply isn't an option,

nights when our ghosts
must rise from their ring of chairs
and hurry the length of the garden,
crowd the kitchen doorway,
and stand closer than our shoulders,
in order to watch the rain.

Yellow Shoes

The only way is to step into yellow Shoes.
A message delivered, as it were in a Bottle,
To the edge of an Ocean of Truth.
Or Sleep, in which case it will come as no Surprise
To note the reach of its fine reticulations.
A concrete Path that runs the length of the Garden
Is simply there to be taken. So we'll take it,
And while it will usher us out through a Gate
Into the Heart of the All-Forgiving West,
It may also, remember, run Elsewhere,
And even Everywhere, too.

Tweedles

Squalls of wind
and sudden gusts of rain.
Peony petals leave their stain
on blue steel samurai armour,

while Dum and Dee
in their lunatic pomp and gear
come jousting either side of the fence
before falling off their giddy-up broomstick chargers
and rolling around in the grass.

Moon-Leaper

There was a lad before now, and the whole trick and talent of him was that he could leap above the moon. But although he could leap above the moon, he could not command the place of his landing. So this is what happened, and is the tale of his three leapings.

The first leap he made, he landed in the innermost court of the King of China. The King was angry at his coming and said, 'Who art thou, lad, to land among us thus?'

'I am Moon-Leaper,' said the lad, 'and give me thy finest porridge!'

'That I will not do,' said the King of China, whereupon the lad took a ploughshare that he had about him and struck off the King's left foot. The foot went springing over the flags of the court, crying in a high and piping voice, 'Restore me! Restore me! And thou shalt have our finest porridge.' So the lad restored the foot, and a bowl of the finest porridge was set before him, and he said, 'Thou art the porridge for me!' and he became the Steward of the Court of the King of China for a year and a day.

The second leap he made, he landed in the midst of the wide timbered hall of the King of All of Norway. The King was having his hair dressed by his women, and was angry at this interruption and said, 'Who art thou, ill-found lad, to land among us thus?'

'I am Moon-Leaper,' said the lad, 'and I am come for the best of thy salmon!'

'That thou shalt never have,' said the King of All of Norway, whereupon the lad took an iron creel from his back and struck the King's nose from his face. The nose lay flapping and twitching by the throne, crying in a pitiful voice, 'Restore me! Restore me! And thou shalt have the best of our salmon.' So the lad restored the nose, and a fine broiled salmon was set before him, and he said, 'Thou art the salmon for me!' and he became the Chamberlain in the wide timbered hall of the King of All of Norway for a year and a day.

The third leap he made, he landed in the Glen of the Blue Glass Castle, where grows an Apple Tree. The Tree shivered in the wind, and a hollow voice boomed forth from the branches and said, 'Who art thou, thou whey-faced lad, to come landing among us thus?'

'I am Moon-Leaper,' said the lad, 'and I am come to take thy daughter!'

'Her thou shalt never take,' said the Tree, whereupon the lad let fly the blue-eyed hawk from his shoulder and it swooped upon the leaves and plucked from them the Only Apple, which it dropped by the side of a stream. The Only Apple went rolling towards the water, crying out in a round voice, 'Restore me! Restore me! And thou shalt have the hand of our daughter.' So the lad restored the Only Apple, and a yellow-haired maiden in a white woollen gown now stood before him, to whom he said, 'Thou art the daughter for me!' and the two of them were married, and a great lineage sprang from their loins, and they reigned in the Glen of the Blue Glass Castle, and for all I know and if they are not dead, are reigning there till this day.

In Poulton Street

Out in the yard at the age of three
she crushed her thumb in the mangle,
the pain and shock of it
spoiling the sight of her eye,
'turning it' the doctor said,
in a phrase from Edwardian medicine
that I do not understand.

It was a yard which soon would hang suspended
below a looming Zeppelin,
lost returning from a raid on Liverpool,
filling the sky with German voices,
now clearly heard in Poulton Street
and therefore in that kitchen
where she kept a bantam hen beneath the sink,
where it was cool, and where her pet dove came
to be fed on the window sill
pink in the cramped sunlight.

When the night came it would invariably come
through this yard and this kitchen
and into a central room behind the shop,
pushing her in with her sister and mother,
between the bird asleep in the white of the dark
and the greased racks of bikes and airguns,
parts for sewing machines.

It was in this square of hissing gaslight
by a flickering evening fire
that her mother, dozing,
broke the kitten's back beneath the runners
of the rocking chair,
blamed herself for years,

and where stored boxes of fireworks
would come to be ignited by a spark
into a cartoon riot of rockets
that nearly killed her, setting her hair alight.

It was here that the stairs ran up steeply
to the room where her mother
had given birth to her alone,
already six months widowed
of a brilliant man, a boilermaker,
owner of ice-skates and a telescope,
a beautiful dancer who died of Bright's Disease,
and where a blue light that was never afterwards doubted
as having been Our Lady
shone at the foot of the bed,
as if with words of comfort.

It was here that she would have lain
the whole of those first few months
while her mother sewed silk shirts for gentlemen,
working an old treadle
for gentlemen whose ladies kept her waiting,
standing once in a hallway to be paid
and hearing through a deliberate door
a mistress saying loudly to her servant
'The woman is ugly', though with slender waist
and streaming auburn hair
her beauty then was almost all she had.

She must have walked home after this
by houses where lawyers and the doctor lived,
Devlin, an Irishman who entertained the opinion
that cancer ran in buildings, not through families,
and once would have lifted her daughter's toenail off
on the back of a soup spoon, except that the child
fled hopping through the open door of his room

the boot and much abuse hurled after her,
all the names

beneath the sun which shone on the part of town
where her grandmother sat in a black silk dress
with a bag of sovereigns at her waist,
to be dipped into like chocolates
in afternoon light that would sometimes get as far

as the back room of the shop,
pushing through streets that in the
Great Town Flood a few years later
in the time of my mother and my grandmother
who used to say 'By the Harry!' and about whom
it is more than ever important to write at this time
were nine feet under water and jammed
when the sea finally retired
with dead sheep sodden luxury
and giant beams that had burst the decks
of a Russian timber ship
newly arrived from St Petersburg.

Giant Forms

1 *Antonio Vivaldi*

The largo from Vivaldi's *Winter*
is said to offer some respite
from the 'biting wind and fallen snow',
but what I always hear is summer rain
being woven on an upright loom in a park.
I sit in my window and the deep cold night
presents its stillness like a plate of country food.
I dwell with giant forms on St Hilary's Day,
And wonder if God can misinterpret music.

2 *William Cowper*

You send to your friends for fish,
or the paper on which
to reply at length to their last.
Believing yourself damned, you act as if
all England's roads and posts are built
to help you spend your love before the night,
but in this you fail. Your advice on gourds
continues to travel the frozen spokes of the wheel.
Our gift of the finny tribe in barrels
still jolts toward your house down stiffened lanes.

3 *A third*

The drunken moon
all mantled in gas
is hanging low in the west.
You've never seen it in that place before
and it startles you at first.

You sway in the frame with golden fumes in your neck
and gape and swoon like some Doctor of the Church.
The best that can be said for you, my friend,
is you don't close the door until you've realised this.

Smoke

Send up some smoke,
tinkers,
your smoke out of India.

Woodsmoke
or dung smoke,
some dry Sanskrit panniers

Burn our piss
with our excrement,
burn up these mattresses

Sting the night with onions,
blind our moon,
our policemen

Smoke our heads in your
kettles, Indians,
gobsquirts of chai on them

Make us weep with your
smoke, you bastards,
keep telling us stories,
keep stitch and
un-stitching our eyes

A Chaplet or Minor Rosary

On a bottle of Xoriguer brought back as a dog-sitting thank you:

How I like it
When the fridge-cold pastry
Sucks up the vinegar
Splashed in the dish

And how I do like it
When the self-same pastry
Asks to be sung to
Befriended by gin

Oh yes they are a pair of demons
When yoked together, gin and cold pastry,
So stay out of the pantry
In case they do you in

I was a teacher once:

A day I remember, forty years ago.
I was reading Persian on a midsummer morning.
She was out at work and I was reading Persian
For I was a teacher and the day was a day
In the middle of the vacation.
Were things really so? Could I ever have been a teacher
Reading Persian on a summer morning?
Or ever have been
So alone in the face of the future,
Putting down the book of Persian
And stepping out to the shop across the road
To buy cigarettes
While the sun moved across
The face of the sky
And the sparrows chirruped 'Fuck!'
In Greek or something?

The fashion for Rumi:

They say he is their favourite poet
But what they're really into
The wankers
Is articulating their middle-class prestige,
Mooning and swooning over words put together
By some cleverdicky creative writing shit
Who works from a crib
And claims to be a Sufi

Bees again:

There were bees in the pudding
I couldn't believe it
And sticks in the pastry
Or do I mean pantry
Whatever I do mean
It just didn't seem right

What kind of person
Would serve one up insects
What host or hostess
Could possibly think it right
To serve up tiny
Things of the "stick" class
And after eleven o'clock at night

Sufficient Unto the Day

Small brown leaf,
tumbled in the February wind.
Nothing much more to add to that,
except perhaps for
'How like a bird,
How very much like a bird.'

Care in the Park

'God' God's pronoun,
own pronoun

to be dispensed with

robed in the empty

majesty of disclosure

even here and now

as a man approaches

with outspread palms

and speech at terrible cost

'Look…
I've got…fucking…
NOTHING, mate'

Matelot

(for Archie Markham)

You can never remember, you say,
as our second glasses usher in
a most unaccountable dreamtime,
whether the word means 'sailor' or 'stool'.
Ah. You must think it possible, then,
that my great great grandfather,
whom I've only just brought into this our conversation,
was possessed of three wooden legs,
and bobbed his way along the main
without benefit of sail, all the way to Antigua.
Or am I misunderstanding you here?
Perhaps you conceive of a British naval vessel
officered by men but crewed by furniture,
a true Ship of Stools. I'd prefer to think so.
Seeing my ancestor
as but one among a whole ship's complement
of forms, benches, balloon-backs, settles,
folding items for use on safari, modified tubs,
casks, slatted garden seats and early forms of deckchair
is clearly very much nicer for me to imagine.
It renders him less egregious, more a part of history.
For what is most important about my forebear
is not the number or nature of his legs
but the fact of his being one among thousands
of items designed or adapted for sitting upon
which were set afloat to combat an evil trade
on the ocean between the Slave Coast and the Brasils.
True, there were those among his older mates
who had fought those damn 'chaises longues', the French,
and hankered after such days of glory still,
but to younger crew like him I sense that it seemed
(I choose to believe that it seemed)
rather more worthwhile, even rather more noble,

to lift out of dark wormy holds
and pile on deck in air as dawn was breaking
or the sun going down their undoubted brothers and sisters
than to bandy splinters with other wooden worlds.
That I've always wanted to visit the Caribbean
is what I was going to say before you started
this nonsense about stools and now you tell me
if I ever do so to be sure to stay
with your sisters in Dominica.
I would really like that, Archie,
I think I would really like that,
at least to judge by the way I already imagine
all of those presently seated around this table
set out instead upon a sudden verandah,
in warmest moonlight, overlooking the sea.

River Traffic

The swing bridge opens.
Autumn sky waves clouds upstream.
Barges, t'other way.

From the Fire Tower

A galvanised aluminium
observation platform
rises, high as a house,
above this heathland
that used to be a bog,
ombrophilous dome
of quaking saturation
and black pools,
necklaced now
in candid bladder campion.

Up here in the wind
is the great ultra-violet
circle of the world,
all that you may happen,
or be compelled, to notice:
a distant kestrel, spires,
a life's few decades
told like beads on a string,
once a cloud which slowly became a tornado.

And down there?
Down there once were tubs
of bright butter preserved, rivalling gold,
below us lay hidden in darkness for centuries
gracefully spiralled envelopes of skin
which before that had been bodies,
before that corpses,
before that respiring men and women
led along trackways
they had helped to build themselves
into the heart of the sun.

Which is where we are now, it almost seems,
come by paths constructed much the same,
on rafts of brushwood,
with pegged and staked side-rails,
moving adder-like
towards the inevitability of here.
So much information
So much data needing to be processed,
and all since the whole damn thing first flared.
Six thousand years for this vanished landscape to build,
fifty to strip it out for garden compost,
a handful to form the arena we utilise now.
All have climbed to the platform today.
All lean out into air and debate the horseflies,
as someone hands a bag of cherries around.
All have noticed, and questioned, and prophesied things.
A darkness so bright we mistake the water for shadow;
day and night and season working like tides
as peat once again begins to submerge the tower;
this very evening, even, and in our absence,
with nightjars come to cruise the habitual dusk.

An Exhortation to Himself

Read no further in old men's books,
Too many of those when young.
Peruse, for preference, green and youthful
Incunabula, aestiva/hiems,
Gnomon-like invite the bright meridian,
Be freshly peeled and newly indicative wand.

Bevis of Hampton

(for Lisa Wastling)

Bevis of Hampton sate upon a hill.
Beneath a tree, on a February day.
The tree it bare both pears and plums,
And all his food was a green goose, oh.

All his meat was a green, green goose
And all his song a greenwood glee,
In which he joined with horse and hound,
Or the which he plucked with his fingers, oh.

Their only song was of Robin Hood
So to sing that then they must agree,
Bevis enhelmed upon the hill.
His creatures either side the tree.

It was cold that day, the day was cold,
And the green, green goose was colder still.
The hound it was that gnawed the bones,
The horse that stood in eternity.

And Bevis? What of him? Alas,
We hold his memory but in dream.
The years have closed above his head,
A grievous thing to have to tell.

His deed before the gate of Rome
Is now forgot, his thousand miles in Tartary,
How faithful dolphins led him once
To golden Rhodes, an island in the sea!

Homeward Bound

On this seemingly endless avenue
it depends upon how you align yourself
with regard to the trees
as to how much exhaustion you feel

For a moment you have but a "single" one on your left
and can see to the very end of the evening,
with no awareness of intervening distance
or what would detract from your effort to be home

A NATURAL HISTORY

(2003)

For love and wisdom are not abstractions, but substance…
and so is everything civil, moral, and spiritual

EMANUEL SWEDENBORG

Il ne trouvait jamais d'autre abri que l'espace

PIERRE REVERDY

Owl and Miner

The owl alights on his shoulder.
All the day-shift she's waited patiently there,
high in the pine that grows hard-by the pit-head.
Waited blinking and dreaming,
and turning the slow escutcheon of her face.
Waited as that which would serve to draw her master
back with songs from his deep Plutonic shades.

Thus it is that he steps from the earth and is greeted.
She furls her wings, and as they set off
on their mile up the darkening lane,
towards the low-banked cloud of the clustering houses,
he starts to sing to her. I see his white smoke.
His breath on the air he casts as if he would net
the voices of ghosts in the empty elder trees.
For it is winter now, and his songs are of winter.
Wind unparcelled across the keen land.
First light snowfall turning black on hedge.
Warren and iron pool and far road-end,
where now the yellow lights begin to come on,
in twos and threes, haltingly, as if to conjure
the stars to commence their stammering nightly speech.

Revisited

Dawn, and the rain just stopping.
In the yard behind the house
an old-fashioned mop bucket
dreams of going to Heaven,
its god a frog with a seventeen-syllable name.
Out on the street, a milkman sits by the kerb
and writes in his book, carefully gripping the stub
of an almost extinguished pencil.
It must be twenty years ago, all this,
and since I can't now remember
why I was awake
I think I shall add one more unit
to these emblems of gathered silence,
quite possibly a cat,
walking with supercilious self-regard
in front of the milk-float,
down the side passage,
and into our paved and private precinct,
there to lap at freshly collected waters,
her front paws raised on the cold brimming margin
of a sacred pool known to her and her alone.

Praying with Kit Smart while Walking to Work

Praise to the grocer,
who learned to read two centuries ago
but still has not mastered
the finer points of orthography.
Weigh him in the balance of praise
and do not find him wanting,
remembering all the while the unsung pain
of those several of us driven beyond despair
by his wrongly apostrophised *carrot's*
(Language Liberation Front,
Communiqué No. 1)

Praise, too, this householder,
whose coal-black dustbin, standing in the street,
carries in white emulsion, not his house number,
but a jubilant exclamation,
Hendrix is God!
Praise him in the letter you'll send
to commend to his keen consideration
some associated propositions:
God is Hendrix...God is even God

Likewise praise the starling,
who cares not a jot
that the wall she alights on
is laden with graffiti,
but lives in the sacrament
of the present moment.
Praise be to starling,
bringing to breeze-blocks
this fine May morning
her vibrant and (enunciate clearly)
jewel-encrusted dagger

Antique Lands

Banal but effective, the bombs.
If not completely so.
After who knows how long
of ice and swirling black night
some things that might still make sense
to a human ghost. In one high dry place,
in slowly returning sunlight,
a guardian statue, gazing out from a cave mouth.
And in another, on the far side of the planet,
a ferocious gatekeeper, brandishing a sword.

At the Gates

The city at dusk, and suddenly autumn.
One last set of lights
before the emptiness finally gathers itself.
Distinctive lead-grey fabrics,
like those of the Roman jars in the Museum.
The bus throbs. In the upstairs saloon
the windows hum like copying machines.
Enough harsh colour gets swept across them
to cause the last of the daylight to be printed.
Futility? Corruption?
A bright green singlet jogs silently along
the one-way system that stretches in front of us.
A linear panel of blue,
on the stone façade of a bank across the road,
records as if on photographic paper
the electric track of the building's passage through time.

As if in Arden

Did I really hear you say that,
all those years ago,
as we went out walking in the summer twilight
the weekend you came to stay?

Could you and I, my wife and infant child,
really have been so carefree that night,
so 'utterly smashed on Diana's poisons'
as we strolled home talking underneath the stars?

A Natural History

You spoke last time we met
of the petrol-coloured sea.
Our discourse began to look up.
All those present had dreams of ocean to tell,
while one of us claimed to have talked at length
with Thomas Hobbes, the author of *Leviathan*.

He'd been dreaming, he supposed,
was only partly convinced.
The summer then had not yet got under weigh
and all of us were desperately looking forward
to things achieving the balance they seem to have now.

What that means to you I can never know
but with me it involves the formal necessity
of the months of May and June, the fact of the gardens
which lie behind the street in which I live.

I can never know.
But I think it possible you will understand
the degree to which one can come to admire
the evenings at this time of year.
The swift-infested swooping of the dusk.
The sliding planes and opalescent
departments of the sky.

Given in Sleep

Half-wild screaming
of white cars on the coast road.
North Sea Province. Now.

Rusting concrete-filled drums
along the harbour wall.
The gull that watches from each.

As if numerous films, books, and
programmes on the wireless
hadn't started this way.

As if gleaming Lübeck and the Hanseatic towns
didn't have their own
entirely similar establishments.

Coasts of Africa 1850

> Deceased for many years was engaged in the suppression of the African slave trade.
>
> Obituary of WILLIAM HENRY HOBDAY,
> *Fleetwood Chronicle*, January 1912

Undo the thong that closes the mouth of the bag.
Spill William Hobday's coins upon the board.
Build from their falling and rocking into silence
the boom of sheets and blocks and the gasp
of a wind that carries the reek of the swamp in its hair.
Hear him sing of home.
Hear him tell the tale of the names of the coasts
on imagined bracelets of turquoise and citrine beads.
Hear him name the white forts.
Summon him now.
Then down in one the glass of yellow bile
that he brings to your side from the quarter deck to hand you.
Watch him carry a *nigger* up from a hold
to save her ulcerous feet from the salt-scoured planks.
Or stand and gaze with him through lidless eyes
at a barque a cable ahead as it jettisons *cargo.*
Summon him here by reciting in a loud voice
the poundage of cannon and shot.
Oh summon him here with the names of carronades,
with those of comrades, with canister and swivel.
Summon him here from *Philomel*, and that this might come to pass
consume in mind's flame his oak tobacco jar,
let flame devour his ribbons and his papers,
construct a pyre and arrange that all his pain
should tumble to ash, with the last of his books about God.
And let there be smoke. And let the smoke
roll out like mercy to bear the sailor home.
Let the smoke caress in the semblance of a breeze
that beach by the Irish Sea where he paddles at evening.

Then let the smoke vanish, except that it should lie
in the mouth of his jug as the froth upon the beer
he's just been out to fetch,
and now, soothed with stern psalms,
is carrying home in his old man's dappled hand.

Far from the Habitations of Men

Multiple exposure,
the living and the dead.
Ghostly tanners
move silently round a hide.
Their spirit knives flash and flense,
as swift as thought, definitive as text.
Talmud forbids the former synagogue
to be put to this trade's uses.
Mayhew's dog-shit collector,
once a child,
was about these streets
till as late as 1950.

Heartland

(i.m. Frank Stansfield)

But whose heart,
since Hitler bombed
the Puseyites out of Sculcoates?
High Explosive, emptier of parishes,
'tumbled' from the bomb-bays.

What need was here of stones,
when sticks it seems
had been thus empowered against bone?
And yet must leave 'old Frank', even until last year,
bent almost double,
for single witness almost, almost even for saint.
Low and unadorned modernity
squats as sheltered housing across
the vanished streets whose names it dares to retain.
St Michael, All the Angels,
Augustine of Hippo, Monica his mother.
'Take and eat,' calls a voice from a silent garden.
'To walk to work the way you are taking now
is to graze among death assemblages,
be nourished by the taphonomy of worship.'

Pastoral

(for Ralf Andtbacka, after his Swedish)

A swollen moon is grazing out on the wold.
Deer stand motionless underneath the trees,
cardboard cut-outs, staring, unwieldy.
Where do you linger, my friend? The hour is late,
and already the farmer has taken to his bed. I, though,
I lie awake and wait for you. Through the yard
pads black cat Lucifer with soft deliberate tread.
Steaming cattle stand and dream in the byre. Lofts groan
with meat and bread, berries, polished fruit. Spilt grain
lines the trackway verges with gold. And all things
are content, all are at rest, sing their small still song
of contentment, and of rest.

The Green Boy

At the moment of dawn
some long-ago May morning
a green boy emerges
glistening from this dock

stands dripping on the side
of this old stone basin,
and as the light breaks
gazes with newly opened eyes

at smoke lying curled
above one or two houses
in the city's huddled circle,
where the thin child servants

of lawyer and apothecary
of mountebank and thief
are up betimes
and about their masters' business

Kurdistan

(for Mahdi Majid Saleh)

You tear a hole in the sky above Iraq
To show me your prohibited country,
Your nation forbidden its name.

Prisoners without lips
Stare sightlessly back from compounds,
At the huge and burning orb of the Sun,
Which cannot avert its gaze.

'Oh my friend, my brother,
Lidless eyes have learned to weep dry tears,

While the single eye of Satan
Bathes endlessly
In the bitter wine of God.'

The Romance of Steam

Sound of a distant train in the midsummer night.
Other ones, though, are too far away to be heard.
Ancient locos, forgotten in sidings and sheds,
flanks glazed with moonlight,
fast asleep in the dark.
A myriad sullen phantoms. Some consumed by rust,
and some let down upon the floor of the ocean.
Those entangled by nature, roped with jungle vines;
the many secreted by artful bandits in caves;
the ones not even arrived at the drawing board yet.
How easy they are to imagine, these silent varieties:
a dreaming ironclad crawling the coast of Honduras,
a blue-grey shunter tumbling through deepest space
with its *gravitas* intact, grazing serenely
the phosphorescent pastures of the stars.

I heard of an engine once
that some Persian railwaymen
had been forced to bury in sand.
Inspecting the line for rocks and bombs
a day ahead of a train being used by the Shah
and fate decrees they derail the thing on a bend,
stumble around for a minute or so with the shock,
check themselves for broken heads and limbs,

then cease to breathe as they realise their predicament.
If I were you, I said to them,
as sheer cold terror began to undress us all,
I'd get it buried, pronto, so they did.
In a big deep hole by the side of the line,
smoothed over the desert surface afterwards,
then hid behind a bush as the tyrant rolled by.
That's all I know. I lost *track* of them after that,
and can only relate the fervour I now employ
to get them back safely to their villages in the hills,
to greet them with bread and salt and coloured scarves,
then sit them down against walls of sun-dried brick
to take no more part in any kind of history.

The Village, or, Festive Schadenfreude

(for Debbie Joy)

Saint Stephen's Day at dusk.
Ropes of light around the village pond.
A muddy island trampled by heavy birds.
A patch of scrub and a sign enjoining
a Merry Christmas, done in coloured bulbs.

It could be worse.
At least there is something to read.

While wife and child and friend
walk slowly to the other end of the water,
he lags behind to peer at a board,
with glossy graphics and 'Heritage' in its title.
A map shows where all the parish chalk pits were,
which are now such a thorn in the County Council's side,
and where, he supposes,
careless townies may still get done to death

by the old Brer Rabbit method, watched by a sepia gaggle
of former village residents. For look,
here in ancient darkening sunlight
stands Disraeli Gardham, attending a horse's head;
and Waxy Oliver, holding court outside a pub,
one of the three still boasted by the village,
its former custom not yet back from the Somme.

The women and child now stop to wait for him
on the bridge along the road, and as he comes up
he can see the severed scarlet head of a goose
bobbing at the margin by their feet.
They haven't noticed, and he's looking forward
to pointing it out to them,
but all it turns out to have been when he gets there
is a crumpled drinks can, seen from an odd angle,
in the half light, from a distance,
through a dead man's eyes, by a fool.

Strangely, though,
there does actually float there, next to the can,
a headless goose torso, which he *hadn't* seen.
It's upside down, and looks about the size
of the one they've been eating for the last couple of days,
which would make it roughly eleven pounds in weight.
There isn't much worth relating after this.
They take a well-kept uphill path,
traverse a field with a fence which they treat
as being electric until they discover
that it's wired with coloured string,
then wander around the village until it gets dark.
Much of interest, certainly,
but their main enjoyment consists in designing
impoverished lives for the modern inhabitants,
while looking in at their windows,
and spinning dark tales about foxes and water birds.

Pedestrianism

Garden furniture.
Single item described.
A terracotta Sun,
nailed to a house-wall,
holds out complacent cupped hands,
presumably for birds to drink from,
but which now, this dry spring morning,
must pick me up and carry me along
as far as the busy main road,
where an elderly woman
is inching along the shop-fronts,
and will not set me down
till two streets further on,
when, in guise of a command,
a cat breaks out from some bushes,
needlessly frightened,
but moving, as everything seems to know how,
quite surefootedly into the past.

Hell on the Ringroad

Out of the vast car park,
away from the huge
pub by the roundabout,
crawls an empty limousine,
the windows of which are of carbon,
for it is surely the Devil's work.

In every tree along its whistling route
a corpse in chains makes loud complaint to an owl
about branches on the tarmac,
or the gibbous lemon moon.

'I was Virgil!' one screams,
'but that was before I was nameless.
Tonight I assist my companion the wind
in his long disconsolate psalms.'

'I was never true!' cries another.
And another, who squats in an iron cage
in the next tree along, probes the front of his face
with a broken biro, as if searching for his mouth.

It's this feral car which invigorates them so.
Passing up and down their line
like the visiting Lord Lieutenant of a shire,
it demands, and gets, the appropriate attention.
The thud of its wheels on the concrete slabs of the road
makes a stately drum, which these scallywags cannot ignore.

Medieval, Somehow

I go to the second-hand bookshop,
to sell an unwanted saucepan.
Three young women sit bathing
in a high wooden tub in the window.
I wait while the man in front of me gets paid
in good English coin for a carrier full of skillets,
then it's the turn of myself and my singular pan.
Two quid. Five quid. Seven.
Timely acceptance serves to prevent
his offer from holing the roof,
but transactions like this
are never so easily ended.
Before I can leave I must taste the subtle pleasure
of watching my only just sold get purchased again.
Which might eventually happen,
'once mine' and 'never mine' together in the mouth
of a sack held open by a brown-robed mendicant,
smilingly there to refurbish a friary kitchen.

On the Grand Tour

A glass of water,
falling from the third-floor window
of a dark and silent Hotel,
smashes itself to bits
on the English word BICYCLES,
done in white paint
on the cobblestones down in the street.

It's the vertical equivalent
of a phrase from one of the night's sung Offices,
being borne on a breeze
from the outskirts of the town.

I'd have thought myself in eighteenth-century Italy
were it not for these phantom bikes. Therefore...

Enter Lord Auchinleck's son,
freshly emerged from the entrance to an entry,
in an act of adjusting his clothes.

Ah! Signor Boswell...

On a torrent of breath I both greet him and implore,
so that twenty months later
– almost, indeed, by express –
there is put in my hand from London
a Famous Opinion, recruited on my behalf.

It will be much to your purpose, Sir,
to regard that candid and anachronistic inscription
which my friend informs me is perplexing you in Italy
not as a problem, but as an insurmountable,
and therefore liberating, difficulty.

Thank you, Learned Doctor.
I had hardly dared hope you could heave your bulk within range
of the necessary post-Newtonian physics.

And so, have you heard from Johnny lately?
To me he sends obsequious Memoranda
from all those small, sad, strewn-about Courts in Germany,
and displays an obsessive interest in prophylactic sheaths,
the which he likes to refer to as his Armour.

Cemetery Clearance

Some kind of scheme, I suppose.
Our Lady of the Bolt-Croppers,
tall and how beautifully trousered,
stands smiling among the stones.
Behind her, in the sere grasses of autumn,
in the low drifting smoke of small fires,
her young men crawl
at her bidding among the dead.
Spirits and wonders!
To whatever is able to will to invest
with such an image of the fitness of things
even this sorry enterprise
honour and praise is for ever abundantly due.

Victorian Angels

(for Ann Clark)

Victorian men
knew that angels were really girls,
albeit girls with wings.
Hence the mooning about,
with downcast glance
and charmingly troubled hair,
in damp September graveyards;
hence the clutching
to tender new-swelling bosom
of silent, baby-sized, lyre.

Victorian women, of course,
knew they had once been girls

but guiltily doubted, the two things are connected,
any past, or present, or future
status as angels.

We agree with them.
Patience and suffering such as theirs,
though yet they cry out for heightened description,
fall outside the angelic experience.

Lives and deaths
in the phallocentric arena
of fathers' and husbands' faces;
the stern implacabilities
of consecrated law;
the agonised fevered brow
of infant after infant;
the terrible, photographed,
wounds of the Crimea.

Now and Then

June sky autumn gale the morning
whirls with blown things.
Plume from pencil thin aluminium stack
goes solo in schoolroom chalk,
light blue for contrast
with the evening before's
already sanctified past.
Of deluge, thunder, devotional lash and roar,
though by the time
the library closed its doors
there was temporary calm
and an almost totally gone west sun

made netherlandish brick,
did old academy's picture rail top
in nervous painterly light,
scooped backhand froth off lime trees in soldierly lines
and rendered the gleaming hospital far over south
into broken insouciant stranger than meaning shadow
of palaeolithic cliff with rainbow now hitting.

To Warm a House

(for Martin and Gail)

Bread. Salt. Wine. Verse. Song.

These gifts we bring,
Ungraced, I fear, by parcel-wrapper's art,
To wish you all
We hope you'll never lack.

Bring here this very night, that is,
To the newest abode
Of your lives' abiding,
Bread and salt,
The one home-baked
The other corner-shopped,
With the very best that Ernest and Julio
Have known how to tread,
Or Bloodaxe to anthologise.

And for song?
Well, Couperin,
To memorialise those lessons
That are only learned among shadows,
Respectfully asking

That they absent themselves tonight,
Unless gifted by guttering candles
To the tired but happy wreckage
Of an admired and fortunate feast.

And now, my friends,
Put back and leave these gifts in carrier bag,
Deliberate to deflect the gaze
Of any wandering petty god
Who may hereabouts flit,
Susceptible to jealousy.
When you wake tomorrow, be reminded
That bread, salt, wine, verse, song
Each in its own way burns and hath sufficiency;
That hearth, heart, love and house,
Your lives and soon to be three lives life,
May all be lit and warmed thereby;
And that this, as now we seat ourselves at your table,
Is what we both, in unsolemn reverence, wish you.

At a Pinch

Our haircuts in the 1950s
allowed our mathematics teachers
(who were often also Methodist preachers)
some interesting ways to reach us.

The art of raising an angry lump
behind the ear of the natural boy
by twisting the short hairs tightly clockwise
(one later confided)
had occupied the whole first year of their studies.

We relied for theory
(he wheezed, his eyes bedimmed by memory)
on a few grand old works one hardly sees today:
the *Pedagogic Gospels*, here ranged in dust,
sweet Euclid's tract *On Manly Punishment.*
And for practice? He smiled.
For that we had what the State, in its wisdom, provided,
and at home, in vacations, our nephews, sometimes our nieces.

For Notes

On a blank leaf
at the end of Janet Maccombich's prayer-book
the following:

'Fairies are just small angels.
Omission from hierarchy inexplicable
(but presumably political).

Our minister does not agree
(surprise?!?)
which makes me think it may even be
sexual.

Old, old difference.
Obedient attendance upon the Word
or culpable wrong-headedness
(for which, alas, he knows as well as I
he will one day answer Elsewhere).'

The remaining contents of the page,
in different ink, and separated from the above
by a thin ruled line, need not detain us long,
though they may perhaps be mentioned:

a simple sum;
some hastily scribbled words (milk? Thursday?);
and a careful sketch of the face of a cat,
peering out of dense foliage,
or perhaps with wings intended to be innumerable.

Chai

Autumn morning.
Ridiculously early.
You break your fast
with dark brown tea and tobacco,
then rest your hands
on the solid kitchen table.
Your feet are 'unstockinged'
as once we used to say.
You glance down at the floor,
then realise how good it can feel
to allow the cold
its claims upon your warmth.

Eight Magpies

(i.m. Lex Barker)

Eight magpies this morning,
trampolining off the bare, sprung cage
of a winter tree,
and chacking away as they did so,
not at all like the grim behaviourists
we're supposed to think animals are,
who would probably take
no joy in this location whatsoever,
the deeply sunk road
of a disused urban branch line,
running below the uneven slabs and silence
of a platform from which, you suddenly tell me,
you were sent to live in the country.

Their Names

The day that Chastity-overcometh-serpents McGowan
was married to Rend-the-veil-of-the-temple Rankeillor
she saw, as if in a vision, and forty years in the future,
their names together on a dark red sandstone column.
The pride she felt! Rend-the-veil, for his part,
and trembling in a like enchantment, blanched as he considered
the cost, to his heirs, of the lettering. Ah, his pale trembling!
As the candle flame that winter afternoon, as the sighing of the minister.
Not known before that as much given to exhalation,
the latter sighed again, and bent his age-dimmed eyes upon the Register.

The Country Bus

Every morning, on board the country bus,
I imagine our forbears deforesting the clay,
amazed how erotic such former wetlands can be.

I've come to divide my time on the journey
between archaeological thoughts about drainage
and idle rehearsals of my sexual history.

At the edge of town there's a girl gets on
who looks as if her people might have graced
this landscape for a couple of thousand years,

where silken channels run between the fields
and upstairs travellers lower their eyes to gaze
through glass and leaflight, at its gently waving cresses.

The House Sitter's Letter

(for Gentian)

Thank you for lending us
your house and your cat
again this year.

We had no right to expect it.

She is called Pebble
and lives off dried food,
but of course you already know this.

And isn't it quiet here!
I feel I could borrow the name off your jar of pickles
and become a Chinese poet!

I would if it wasn't Woh Hup.

Woh Hup...

Wasn't he the one
who dipped his drunken hair in ink
and filled a wall in the house of a friend
with swirling vermilion carp?

Actually
I'm much improved of late
and hardly batted an eyelid earlier on.
I don't say I approve
of cotton shirts behaving like that
in the humid midnight wind
but I'm assured I've come a long way.

Whereas *you*, of course,
have *gone* a long way. Away.
Away to your African drumming in Dumfries,
and look, I don't want you to
worry and spoil your retreat
but between you and me,
I think it's Pebble who's the nervous one.
You should see the way she behaves when it thunders,
you really should.

Not the Noise of the World

Not the noise of the world.
In the body of the whale
the system booms and roars
like pipework in
a broken down hotel.

Not its spurious stillness.
In the limestone forest,
a soft declension
of calcined birds into ash.

No, not these,
but the complementarities,
brought and sought,
of sound and silence,
penitence and grace.

Birdsong occurring as gift in the vacuum
of the inter-canonical hours.

The silence made here,
conspired with here tonight,
as the silence of which
all liturgies are afraid.

The New Badge

And then, overnight, a new Badge appears,
on all the city's street furniture.

In the process of standing round in the snow,
discussing what this might mean, the citizens discover
that they can't remember what the old one looked like.

Some say a barge.
Others an owl.
Yet others a quiver of wands.

The argument swirls back and forth all day.
They argue about it until the candid squares
grow sick and tired of reflecting their azure faces,
they argue about it until they agree to agree,
but only because darkness is falling,
that it used to be a bed.

The city sleeps.

From shortly after two in the morning, however,
here and there the lights begin to come on.
People are waking up and drowsily finding
that they didn't notice what the new badge looked like.

Soon the city is ablaze with the great question.
The light from a million windows
turns the blizzard into a jazz-tune.

It is truly eldritch, this conclave of colourful panes
met *con vibrato* to decide a matter of emblems.
The erotic dark red ones
are sticking out for it being a rose on a plate,

while the yellow, pastel, lace-trimmed
and sickly phosphorescent factions
bring hundreds of years of the city's story to bear
on behalf of the claim of a riderless horse in a pond.

It is immensely tiring, this free and untrammeled debate
and come the dawn has wearied all its participants.

If you'll accept that an elemental force
which for months has raged among the towering heights
of a great metropolis can succumb to boredom,
and express that boredom suddenly with a yawn,
then consider this to have happened.

The storm subsides.
The citizens recover a fitful sleep.
When morning finally breaks
a hundred thousand chiliocosms of snowflakes
graze quietly in the parks,
for all the world as if they enjoyed carte blanche.

Nowhere Near

Nowhere near.
No dream as good as this
for many a year.
But others dream too
and some of them are friends

who rise from the communion rail
and walk down to the river,
where the sun is just coming up
and nothing need be said

except, later,
knowing someone who lives
down by this pier
makes us wonder
whether we ought not to ring her

Tailor in a Landscape

(a poem for translation into French)

A tailor who lives by a slowly winding river
tells me all about the three-headed dog
which for years has prefigured
every one of his dreams.

Whatever their content, he says.

As if a single title-page
should serve for every book.

Then he falls silent again.

It's late afternoon
and the time has come to leave.
The rain is thinking of stopping
but the sky can't be bothered to clear.
The dark wet boles of many willow trees
get stuck in the teeth of the light.

I have far to go.
And soon it will be evening.

I ask myself just what it must be like
to be a tailor and live by a river,
and be driven to quiet frenzy
by a polycephalous hound,
and always have to be seeking out
the best of the worsening light.

I can't stop thinking of his life going on in my absence.

There's the sound of a bell.
A far-off train.
The cries of marshbirds.

I imagine the rise and fall of his hand
in the darkening meadow behind me.

And watch with renewed intent my sodden shoes,
as they faithfully precede me through the grass.

Thus

The park lawn lifts
at a sudden command
its beach of blue-grey cobbles
high above the trees

A dog runs forward barking
through the cold conjubilant air and birds
of a springlike winter morning

In Silence

Dark chopping seas.

Dark smoke laid out
in lines for miles astern.

A flag flapping brightly
on a distant coaling station.

The impossible light
of degraded film stock,
flickering over a fleet.

Queen Victoria's Chaffinch

Her last courtier,
a bright male chaffinch from a neighbouring tree,
bids adieu to her with song,
quits her young crowned head
then launches itself down the line of her gaze
across the morning park,
towards the café and toilets.

Were it now to land upon Albert,
who stands aloft at some small distance,
one hand in the breast of his frock coat,
one leg purposefully advanced
and slightly flexed at the knee,
we might believe this blithe spirit drawn
by tractor beams contrived of princely desire,
or following lambent atomic flight paths
seen only by birds, projected by cold marble eyes.

But it doesn't. They do not even face each other.
The Consort has his back towards the Queen,
and she in turn is seated upfield of him,
compelled to watch what she does not care to observe.
They have been like this for one hundred and forty years,
and no one round here is quite sure that they understand why.

Not that our claim upon the fantastic
should in any way be lessened by the fact
of civic ornament thus churlishly disposed.
The chaffinch flies and sings, flies and sings
at will through the rippling air,
and if, as we hereabouts choose to maintain,
our statues have been invested with the right
to leave their plinths on the stroke of midnight,
and house souls again for the durance of the chimes,
then... ah, what then? Surely there will be time, just once,
for them to find each other, for fingertips to touch,
for moonlight on dew-spangled grass
to reflect itself in her eyes, for softly murmured words?

'Albert, my dear. It has been so very long.'

'Liebchen, these spacious gardens of the dark
are graced by your white beauty, and by day the songbird
trills homage around your throne.'

Giant Forms

Tonight you imagine a frost-giant,
looking in at your window
through curtains not given
the care they really deserve.

This will take place
as the day first breaks into light,
so that what your guest will attend to
will be simply your sleeping form.

With feet fast in the yard,
and hair fanned like frozen spray against the roof,
it will stoop a little to watch you,
will have to, being a giant.

It will be scrupulously cold,
its face devoid of all but directed attention,
its eyes of all but unconcerned enquiry.
And it will watch you in ways
you can not understand,

and which even to try to picture to yourself
will be only to model and burn
your Chaos Fear in paper,
then mix its ashes with urine
to scatter upon the fields.

For which reason, do not do so.
Deprive yourself of this pleasure.
If it can "see warmth", like a cat,
or soft white bone in the charcoal of the flesh,
or the flux of phosphors in a blinding particle stream,
what is this to you? Your hand upon the wheel

can never slow the cycles of ice and fire
or empire be prolonged by even a single day.

Sleep on, then. There is no transaction between you.
Active or passive. Actual or possible.
It will not enter your sleeping as a dream
or stir your limbs with a restlessness or fever.
Sleep on. Let giant forms observe you as they may,
or as they may care to. At dawn and with your blessing.
Through all the days and all the nights which remain.

From the Top Floor   of the Library

Not an ivory tower   these afternoons in spring
but an engine for serving   the rarely glimpsed horizon
an alembic for distilling   liquid essences
from the smell of dusty   window glass
an observation point   akin to those
on the ramparts of Heaven   from which to look out
and see that things are interesting   swaying sanctum
of hermetic susurration   great metropolitan
of the realm of far below   and its
sweet-wrapper whirlpooling   silence
great lord   in the gun-metal air
of drunks who daily   stumble the perimeter
addressing themselves incoherently to bastards

Solarised

At last I get to walk
below the high cliffs,
along the black sand.
And let me tell you something.
It is not as we expected.
My feet print white,
and every step I take
adds itself to a distance which stretches
before me, instead of behind,
taking me back to places
I have never been
but can never quite forget.
Where I find myself now,
it is a west-facing bay
where sanderlings run on the shore,
and the fractured dazzle of sea and sky
is a myriad tiny flint crescents,
conchoidal débitage
from some ongoing work of the Sun.
Are you with me thus far? No matter.
You will be soon, and in the meantime
all you may do is attend.
The rocks are still warm.
The path we never took that day
still stretches round the headland.
In a little while, there will step from the waves
entirely appropriate forms, darkly illumined,
bearing that of which I cannot yet speak,
but names perhaps, and artefacts, and graces.

The Valley Floor

Winter's liquid green
fields from the top of this bus,
'flasks', for the word is flat enough,
of an almost chemical joy.
And therefore almost illicit.
The penniless morning hare,
leaping like a broken-backed cat
across these glacial gravels,
will end up getting shot if she's not careful.
And truly, there is that which would have us travel
behind blacked-out windows if it had its way,
in necessary blindfolds, or even without our eyes.

Therefore Choose Life

It may have been the night I dreamed the machine code
that I took my latest step along the road
of realising just how strange
whatever it is that is going on here *is*.
I stood before the familiar inner screen,
the one that is both self and not-self,
and maybe also neither,
and watched as there slowly scrolled, unrolled,
an array of symbols principally composed
of bars and filled circles,
a kind of fat Morse, in all the primary colours.
And that's about it. In fact, its importance seems to reside
in the paucity of what there remains to say:
I was not amazed.

I don't remember any terminating transition.
That which I stood and watched did not require
me in any way to adopt a different posture.

THAT OLD-TIME RELIGION

(1994)

Things we make up out of language turn into common property

ROY FISHER

Still, individual culture is also something

ARTHUR HUGH CLOUGH

The Shore

A minute past noon,
and deeply cold on the shore.
The sun with its rare but un-marvellous halo
starts climbing back down the sky.
The air stills. Wind lies over field
like a razor held above a leather strop.
The beach is locked and hard.
Its uncut gems, and small round leaves
like patinated coins,
it keeps beneath plate glass.
How empty things are.
The cliff behind us acts from some notion of presence,
but very faintly, like a host of spirits
crowding to sip at a pool.
The world of phenomena gathers at the surface
of a system of unity powered by emptiness.
Hills. River. Line of winter farms.
A barge coming down the navigable channel
from somewhere inland, with nothing in its hold.

Passing the Park

(for Genny Rahtz)

I drive by the park
on a bright mid-winter morning.
It's just before lunch,
the car is falling to bits.
Trees conceal
a lake with water-birds.
There issue the sounds
of its undivided nature.
For once, it seems,
there is nothing at all to decide.
A simple song of impoverishment
is streaming like warmth
from the surface of the planet.
Up on the roof of the lodge by the gate
the cups of an anemometer
are turning round in the wind.

The Old Masters

Our lives are short,
and those who taught us have died.
They have taken into Sheol
their facial tics and their jokes.
Their nicknames now
are breathed beneath the ground,
with their black gowns flying
they stalk the touchlines of Hell.

Who pulls down on the brim of his cap
to such as these ones now?
Or who calls their names,
at the going down of the day?
They are come to nothing,
these mighty men of old,
are as air between goalposts
or chalk in the cracks of the floor.
For their classrooms know them not,
and neither are their voices heard in the Hall.
From *Big Field*, *Majuba* and *Spionkop*
their cries have long been carried by the wind.
They have all gone home,
and all the desks which remembered them are burned.
They have bent to their bike-clips at a quarter past four
and left the bike-sheds emptied of their bikes.
Their names are gone up in smoke.
Their insignia have vanished.
The teeth of them have been loosened on their pipes
and all their briefcases finally come unstitched.
Their day is over.
Their sum works out at nought.
From morning's blackboard the evening has erased
their map of the world, their scribbled declension of *ego*.
They have gone down into the grave-mouth and taken
their wartime ranks and all their fountain pens.
And now there are none alive which are like them.
And only their mark-books remain.

A Troubadour

O my lady, your delectable bottom,
pressed to the window-glass in the ancient tower,
defies the Heavens, and makes counterfeit the Moon.
Have mercy on your serving-man, my Lady,
if only for this, that in inventing you
your heretic may have grievous need of your boon.

Winter Quarters

(for Bryan Sitch)

I watched my letter go. Until that man
got lost inside the glen I held my breath.
When heads on poles above the double gates
all sighed at once, 'Oh heads,' I thought,
'I had not known you were friends.'

Then down from the wind. The thing was done.
My three good names in gracile coal-black hand
were gone from me, were going through slanting rain.
Each step I took across the levelled ground
was matched by one that bore my soul away.

In my room I ordered fire. At my command
a servant tended winter's blackened stones.
Then all night long I watched the flames aspire.
In wooden walls, to sit and watch wood burn,
was all Love wanted, all it knew of home.

Part of the Bridge

(for Robin Moore)

The enormous mentality
of the south bank abutment's
embedded concrete block
is not impassive,
though it copes with the westering sun
as remorselessly as any god with petitions.

It is not to be blamed for its size,
its faces textured with jutting tablets, grooves,
or even our dear conviction that mass,
when sheer enough, moves over into sentience.

To enter its zone on an evening in July
is to speak the word temple
in as emptiness-sanctioned a voice
as is used among the mountains;

to hear what it does with the fabulations of air,
that move in its precinct like spirits of ancient birds,
is to know both the paradox, and the stimulus, of its pity.

At North Villa

Flakes of white ash.
Then a telegram about them.

No such thing any more.
Good reason to make this "historical".

Such a message in 1902, then,
being read by a person standing at a window,
a mature person of sober religion and tastes.

It was the middle of that morning.
Wet gusts of wind were engaged in tearing
blossom from trees in his kerchief-sized orchard.
Somewhere deep in the house
a domestic servant was singing *con gusto*
her polystanzaic ballades.

Four posts a day in 1902
plus special delivery of parcels and telegrams.

To 'flakes of white ash' he decided he would reply
with 'a bushel of garden loam',
but could not imagine to whom
this would seem the appropriate courtesy.
An answer had almost suggested itself
when terrific commotion in process of being let loose
directly outside his room
made him open his door to find that *somehow or other*
a large wet dog had entered from the street
and was gaily disturbing with its wagging extremity
the contents of the hall umbrella stand.

The sound of iron-shod sticks being thus re-arranged
within the stand's rectangular tin tray

was a tympany he perceived he could do without.
Water shaken from the layered capes
of his housekeeper's shoulder, as she pirouetted and shooed,
determined him likewise to enter his study again.
His cabinet. The word had very power to soothe him,
and considering this he wiped his aids to vision
while taking the first of the dozen myopic steps
which would bring him back to his table,
a handsome affair of mahogany and leather
which being arrived at he returned his lamps to his nose
and bent to retrieve the missive concerning white ash.

He closed his eyes. He breathed out slowly.
He opened his eyes. And then he stooped again.
Failing to find it where memory told him it lay,
on the blotter, he searched with mounting frustration
the carpet, the mantelpiece, the window seat,
and behind the ormolu statuette of Anubis.
Being the kind of fellow he was
the relocation of that mislaid piece of intelligence
could have swelled in import till it engendered the undesirable,
but as it happened it was scarcely more than an hour
before his hand encountered, in that portion of his jacket
to which he had lately returned his Irish lawn,
a crumpled and now quite sodden piece of paper
which had clearly seen service between someone's finger and thumb.
Sighs fought with smiles, then, awarding his normally gathered countenance
a certain vigour, a wind in the unmown grass of a modest orchard,
a *canzone* defying an established compendage of doors.

He sat down.
Restoring the wire as best he could to its shape
he recalled how washing and shaving with the dawn
he'd looked forward to nothing more than a day with his coins.
But now all this.
Apple blossom pasted to the glass,

a mysterious telegram,
the speed with which he had not reached
an ungainsayable answer,
the wet black dog in his hall.

It was almost as if the house had decided
no longer to do without him, and to command his attention
was plucking his sleeve with what fingers it could form
from the strangeness of days and its own intelligence.
He did not feel afraid, he thought, then at once felt afraid
that the notion had entered his head. Who could tell now
what the rest of the daylight might hold?
Or by nightfall be lying
beneath his diarist's hand? Not *he*, he knew,
and began to rise by instinct from his chair,
who had dwelled in North Villa for nigh on forty years,
a second before he would hear the luncheon bell sound.

An Egregious Talent

Arse-ripping farts were his speciality,
with which he would signal surprise, enquiry,
distaste, *ennui*, and contempt
with equal facility.

He did not suffer fools gladly,
and the condescending HARRUMPH
with which he was used to greet imbecility
made him feared throughout Europe, in his time, apparently.

A Moment's Reflection

The books, the booze,
the more than a third
of a million cigarettes.

The terrible need to enthuse.

If you'd not been yourself
you might have kept pets,
but you are, haven't you heard?

It's not as if life were stored on a shelf
and all you had to do was reach down
some walls of pale blue plaster,
a plump satin heart, a piece of alabaster.

You're not around to choose.

You'd hardly be sitting here
costing the vital parts
of this most costly of all arts
if you'd had a say in the matter, now would you?

The Gun

(for Lex Barker)

I found a gun in a field, barrel burst,
stock rotted away. I took it home
and removed the worst of the rust with a brush,
standing at night on the kitchen doorstep.
I used to dream about guns,
while sleeping I mean,
but gradually that stopped happening to me.
I don't know why I brought it home that day,
I suppose it seemed not *any* piece of scrap,
but all it does is lie by the back door,
unremarked by all who come to the house.
No one seems to notice this old gun,
but if I tell them its story they all act the same,
must see it, hold it, express delight at my luck.
In some odd way the thing has become a touchstone,
though of what is proving difficult to tell.
I suspect it has helped me to love my friends
more nearly than before, if that were possible,
for I've shewn it to several now, and so far none of them
has failed to wonder if it might have murdered someone.

The Shorter 'Life'

I loved the rain,
but always suffered badly
from post-pluvial *tristesse*.

My best wet afternoon was in the mouth
of a disused railway tunnel,
behind me the mile-long carbon-encrusted dark.

That Old-Time Religion

(for Gordon Ostler)

God and His angels stroll in the garden
before turning in for the night.
They've adopted the style
of rich and gifted young Englishmen this evening
and also, bizarrely even for them, decided that they'll speak
in nothing but Sumerian to each other
which all are agreed was a truly heavenly language.

It isn't long before God starts boasting,
in Sumerian of course, that He's the only Being He knows
Who knows by heart *The Bothie of Tober-na-Vuolich*,
and is about to prove it when Lucifer intercedes
to make the points that

a) they've all agreed to speak Sumerian, which was never the
tongue of that estimable poem, and that unless He wants to
pay the usual forfeit, which wouldn't really be consonant
with His divinity, He'd better give up the idea;

b) should He decide to do it into
instantaneous and perfect Sumerian metres,
a feat of which they're all aware He's capable,
He wouldn't be proving His grasp of the original
and would run the risk of them thinking Him a show-off;

& c) since He, God, and not Arthur Hugh Clough must be regarded
as the only true author of *The Bothie*, as of all things,
he, Satan, doesn't see what the point of it would be anyway.

In the silence which follows the Creator is keenly aware
of the voice of the nightingale, then murmurs of consensus,
then much delighted laughter from the angels.

Lucifer bows.

The nightingale stops singing.

God sighs. He could really do without these bitches sometimes
but *then* where would He be?

As if to answer this question to Himself
He withdraws to the farthest reaches of the garden
and leans on the parapet, smoking in fitful gloom,
for what seems like an eternity.
He lights each gasper from the butt of His last
then flicks the glowing end far into the dark,
displeased at His foreknowledge of where it will fall.
To KNOW what His more intelligent creatures have thought
of these lights that appear in August out of Perseus
and not to have disabused them of it, as He's always meant to,
is unforgivable. He gazes in their direction in the dark
and gives them His Word that soon He will change all that,
silent at first, then whispered, then *shouted* in Sumerian.

In a Gothic Yard

(for George Messo)

The tables here are the upturned hooves
of ruined equestrian statues.

The floor is unraked sand,
the service nothing to speak of.

We wait for our foaming maplewood bowls
(of mare's milk, sometimes blood)
and pass an hour attempting to bring to mind,
out of courteous silence,
the plashing of civic fountains.

Knowing that a fountain was not a god,
or a sign denoting a brothel,
has become a badge of learning,
a certain distinction of class.

The foolish and unkempt are coming to think
of bronze as a kind of stone,
pour drinks for horsemen inverted under the ground.

At Her Grinding-Stone

Something about the land.
As if it had taken her elbow, aside,
to tell her an unwanted secret.
The land itself. The sun's high
wheel at noon-tide,
the rutted lane behind the circular houses,
as if the next lot's god had been spotted
sleeping drunk beneath a hedge,
that kind of time-wasting rumour.

Something to do with her worth.
As if all ways of being wife or daughter,
now and forever, had been dreamed at the edge of a field.
Her grinding-stone. Her going down
to the spring-fed pools in the mire,
the stones of her hearth, her raftered pharmacopoeia,
as if the woods had sidled close together
to pronounce her name with another's, most shaming whisper,
most insolent rumour of all.

Words for a Sundial

Approach not me,
but enquire instead
of the great god Fuck,
who almost certainly knows.

Topographical Note

The farmhouses here have no front doors,
just collections of side and back entrances.
They're surrounded by unkempt hedges alive with birds,
and their tenants sit in parlours deep inside them
and stare at walls hung with paintings of fishes and fruit.

In My Kitchen

Boots on last week's newspaper,
flakes of mud on the floor

First to look into freshly opened tomb,
at withered garlands,
plaster fallen from ceiling

Only known as pictograms till now
in texts to do with dusk

But now we have seen the real thing
and how black they are
and how much like our own boots

A Letter to an Editor

(for John Osborne)

Dear Sir
thank you for your letter
asking for some poems
and offering to pay me for them
but I haven't got any left.

I could really have done with
a cheque for £42
but there it is.

I've been working on one
about a hare breaking out
from a square of long grass
beneath an electricity pylon
then vanishing like cold light
across a level arable field
but it isn't finished yet
so I hardly feel that I'm in a position
to be able to let you see it.

I've got it to the point now
where I'm totally clear in my mind
about how that kind of event
is characterised by its emptiness,
gains birth in the void etcetera,
but can't yet resolve in formal terms the equation
between the ogre-bestridden farm in question
and dark wet nights of the kind on which
it forcibly enters my head.

Alas. With 38 quid I could have added to my library
of monographs on Roman pottery
of the first to fourth century,

the structured retrieval of which from the ploughsoil
was my only reason for being
in the middle of that field in the first place.

Still. There we have it.
It occurs to me, by the way, and if it's any help,
that should my inability to deliver the goods on this occasion
seriously inconvenience your 'Margoulis K. Grolsz issue' plans
then a dozen punctuation marks and a few bright nouns
aspersed on an otherwise utterly blank white page
with my name at the top of it
would probably go unquestioned by your readers
and a very long way toward solving both our problems.
We might thus bring down two birds with one handful of gravel
and payment on a *pro rata* basis would of course be acceptable.

You will be aware, I feel sure, that my friendship with Grolsz
WAS OF THE CLOSEST
and only brought to an end by the voice that boomed 'COME!'
on the banks of the Shatt al Bilharz a dozen years ago now.
He never spoke less than highly of my *oeuvre*
and indeed would abjure me never to accept
less than twenty for a poem, so I think it would be a pity
if the fact that I temporarily haven't got any
were to be used as an excuse
to exclude me from this *Festschrift*.

If I could have finished the other thing
then I know you would have admired the way I dealt
with the need I feel to envisage familiar farms
as tenurial units which continue to sprawl on the land
during midnight downpours even when I'm not present,
but I couldn't, so there's no point continuing in this vein
and upsetting myself with thoughts of the postal order for a
fairly substantial sum which I'm certain you would have agreed
with me that it merited.

ANYWAY,

let me know soon what you think of my simple proposal,
hasten to be assured of the importance I have always attached
to my association with your excellent magazine,
and should you see Jaroslaw please stress quite forcibly to him
that the next time he uses one of my lines without
acknowledgement he'll be liable to find
that dawn is not the only thing that goes off like a gun,
the implication being that guns *sensu stricto*
have also been known to act in this way on occasion.

I await your reply with fervent anticipation
and in the meantime, Sir, have the honour to remain,
as ever, and as indigently, one who must be accounted
the foremost among your admirers, namely

The Cartoon Version

Two o'clock again, and the afternoon rains begin.
The longest wet summer of my getting much longer life
runs *amok* on the roof of the shack in which I work,
a long low unit stranded in the claylands,
where archaeologists get what they deserve
and the County Council pastures its yellow snowploughs.
The fertile *ennui* of this pottery researcher
knows no bounds on a Thursday afternoon,
and nor does the glistening god in a *sarong*
who leans from the crown of his swaying palm tree
to peer through my, to him, translucent roof
at these tables laid out with broken potsherds galore.
'Ee,' he says, 'Ah can allus tell
when *tha*'s been doin' t'bloody washin' up,'
then flies back to his jungle heaven and his girls,
to recite an elegant Sanskrit stanza about me
and enjoy their giggling disbelief at his tales.

The Coffin Factory

(for James Booth)

I work next door to a coffin factory.
Offcuts of veneer get blown from its yard
by playful zephyrs, then proceed to slither around
in the gutters and dusty grass
of our semi-industrial suburb.
Only last week, a two-metre strip of the stuff
molested my ankles on the bridge across the canal
so that suddenly I found myself engaging
in a curious ritual bound, a hero-leap,
to arrive on the other side of the stream
in a shower of grits and small gravels.
Lots of things offer to help me narrate this event
(dogs, serpents, land-adapted conger eels and so on)
but I'm tempted most to employ those dragon-banners
which Ammianus describes as having been borne
by the household troops of the Emperor Constantius
when he made his vicennial advent into Rome.
Their gaping mouths were so constructed, he tells,
as to hiss and roar in the breeze occasioned
by each horse's forward momentum, *so I can't help thinking*
that if some of them had escaped from their jewelled shafts
and gained the ground that day, learning to live and breed there
and become a part of the European fauna,
then it might well have been one of their offspring that attacked me,
sixteen hundred years later,
just beyond the gates of the coffin factory.

The Bear (The Sofas)

There was once a bear who longed to be a sofa.

The fact that he wasn't had caused him untold *angst*.

The ultimate day of his lonely life, however,
saw him find himself in a place among some rocks.

It was a natural amphitheatre, an Olympian court
on the razor-sharp circumference of which
a solemn council of *Achieved Furniture Bears*
was perched in down-gazing silence.

It was a cornucopia.

Grapes depended from vines,
which attempted to strangle branches;
honey dripped from the mouths of cool stone jars,
which unseen folk had wedged in the forks of elm trees;
ants as proud and muscle-bound as roosters
ran willy-nilly about the floor of the pit,
to consemble their *braggadocio* with the dawn.

He was overjoyed, this bear who longed to be sat upon.

'I'm about to become a Chesterfield,' he bellowed,
a piety which, untrue as it almost immediately transpired,
the fierce crags in their resolute sympathy
would bruit for a thousand years, *diminuendo*.

The Devil on Holiday

(for Jules Smith)

Satan gets the day off.
And go home early this afternoon as well, says the Boss.
See the world. Walk about in the sun.
I can manage on my own. *Besides, you deserve it.*

Satan doesn't argue. He's been tired, lately.
He feels like a worn-out guy in his middle forties,
in 1940s America, maybe on an August day
of immoderate humour, a single thud from the solar hammer
on a city whose sidewalks, underneath the hoof,
are of preternatural width and adamantine hardness,
and yea this city is the capital of a Beef State,
or it lies like a rock too big to be moved from a field.

OK Boss, says Satan. He is a worn-out old newshound,
and to this kind of news you can only respond with OKs,
so he takes his grey face, his grey trilby, and his
slab-like Robert Mitchum *Weltschmerz* and hooded eyes
out through the outer doors of *Pan Galactic Fantasy Comics Inc.*,
past the iced water and down to the burning street.

Is there a place called Duluth?

Or was there, maybe? Or shall there yet be one?

Satan doesn't know. He's never been to America,
has only the vaguest idea which planet it's on,
so he doesn't reply to himself, just knits his brows
as the trillion always accessible bites of data
begin to buzz like the flies he is held to be Lord of,
and there builds in his skull yet another consuming *Gestalt*.

So much for Intro. *You deserve no less.*
But meanwhile Satan is walking home

on that necklace of palm-fringed plazas which here in Duluth
is draped round the throat of the harbour, and we hurry to catch him up.

Which will not, as it happens, be difficult,
for Satan has stopped to think, and what he is thinking is
Shit, man, his apartment's in Sant' Angelo,
up on The Heights, not down here in Little Cuba
where even the fuckin' *Don't Walk* signs smell of cod
and for fuckssake how can he be so fuckin' stupid
as to've taken a left on Ninth instead of a right on Firestone?

Well, only Satan and one other Ineffably Plastic Entity
might care to answer that one, reader, but what you and I
are inexorably *into* is knowing what happens next,
not waiting for some bejewelled turtle
which swims in the World Ocean
and surfaces only once every million years
to come up with its head through the hole
of the plastic toilet seat which also apparently
floats about on said Ocean, so what I suggest is this,
speaking to Satan now, let us skip over
your bitter little self-deprecations
and catch you up in the gym.

Right. Fernando's Gym.

Five floors up in a brownstone on Sweet Street.

Punchbag. Wallbars. Horse. Ring that reminds the visitor
of one of those white-fenced graveyards out on the prairie,
kind you got put in if you died on a wagon train.
Temple of manly arts. Sanctum of sweat and jock-itch.
Not really Satan's preferred kind of *locus*.

Except for one thing.

It is cool.

Surprising as this information might seem, it is true.
It is the coolest gym in Duluth. The coolest place
that Satan has never been to. For present purposes,
it is the coolest place of all.

We deserve this, Satan. Yes.
And what we shall do to enjoy our well-deserved coolth
is first to bless the mishap and wrong left taken
which brought us to this den; second, to complete,
before mounting of stairs is over
the donning of The Discreetly Invisible Cloak;
and third, just to make sure,
send Morpheus the sleepy slave before us,
by breathing upon to entomb the inhabitants' eyes.

It is done.
Satan can stand in the door of the exercise hall
without fear of recognition. He casts about.
All men. Fernando himself, it must be,
towel round his neck. A white Caucasian baker,
doing a bootlace up. Black guy asleep on a broom.
Thank goodness for that.
No need to take his bifurcated cock
(in two of his hands to wank)
need be felt on this occasion.
Things are looking up. All he has to do
is bask in low temperatures, stroll around
in a comfy realm that is Heaven, compared to Duluth,
explore the john,
and enjoy himself until he begins to get bored.

And yet.
                Already something is wrong.

Satan, still invisible, grows immense inside his wrath.

Fernando turns into a puddle,
the baker a last week's copy of *The West Duluth Encounter*,
the sweeper a baby again, crawling about on the floor.

PANG. *It is not deserved.* PANG, PANG...

Satanic Majesty sweeps to the farthest reach
of the now explicably charred but still chilly gymnasium
and looks out through the fire-escape door, ajar,
right into the furnace that is the sky above Duluth.

PANG.
A kid in a wheelchair, maybe Fernando's boy,
has been parked on the edge of the rusty aerial platform
and is shooting steel balls at a can on the much lower roof
of the building across the street. Satan's eyes narrow.
He imagines becoming a fly of such dark size and weight
that by lifting the bright red brake at the back
of the boy's old-fashioned chair he'll cause a propulsive arc
that will end in a shower of edible snails on the sidewalk,
maybe make the papers.
He becomes this fly.

And now something incredible happens.

Instead of launching the child without delay
he decides a look at the face will be in order
so projects himself slowly down the kid's line of sight,
but a little above it,
thirty yards before dropping and starting to turn.

The boy is blind, as well. The bloated king of the *Diptera*
is aware of this even as he holds the burning air, spins,
and begins to come back up the flight path to the gantry.

So how can the kid take aim? Satan stops in mid-air.

I manage OK I guess.

It's as if the kid
is speaking inside his head, without permission,
in a voice he handles lazily, as one might a cattle-prod.
Satan stares at him. He feels tired.
He seems to be walking inside a blue steel tube
in phosphorescent light, going somewhere,
towards an infant at play by the side of a pool,
a tableau that gets repeated again and again,
so that each time Satan passes overhead the same things recur,
the baby disappears and the pool has become
a sodden page of newsprint, ENJOY
in six-inch headlines of the banner variety
YOUR SUMMER IN DULUTH.

When Satan re-assembles, he is walking north on Firestone.
Feeling good. Organising a complex beat
from the rhythms of two of his hearts. Jiving.
He isn't accustomed to feeling this kind of good.
It must be what happens when you find you've done the right thing.
Not like him to allow himself to be gooked
in the multi-faceted eye, *No Sir!*, the giving of treats
a little out of character perhaps,
but then sometimes enough is enough, destruction, mayhem,
especially that black guy... baby rather...
Satan starts to laugh,
and laughing makes him feel so good that he brings a *third* heart in,
and now an intricate music makes flowers fall from the sky:
tulips, roses, foxgloves, colombines, carnations,
daisies, bugloss, borage, many little blue stars.
And then a fourth. The sidewalk looks like a Persian carpet
or the scene of an outrage inside an eclectic florist's.
Satan looks up. A guy who smells a bit like freshly baked bread
has just stepped out of a doorway, cap in one hand,
wiping his gleaming brow with the back of the other
and asking Satan
what he makes of all these preposterous flowers, Mac?

Satan considers his answer. The guy thinks, Jesus,
I'd like to punch this bastard on the nose,
and I don't know why,
but he takes a single step forwards, just the same.

Satan looks at him. There plays on his face the most courteous of smiles.

I'm on holiday, he says. *Besides, the kid deserved it.*

On Crete or Somewhere

(for Sam Milne)

The peasant here, before the Second World War,
was wont to reckon the distance between ravines
in terms of the number of acrid cigarettes
he would need upon the journey.

To the edge of that darkness a score.
The outcrop yonder then nine.
Thousand on thousand my friend.

He used to move through upland fields of stone
on the back of donkey or mule; it was often winter;
his saturnine and unrelenting ways
were marked by chains of smoke in the lifeless air,
entwined with those left by brigands, gendarmes,
priests who buttoned their beards beneath their coats.

Sitting Propped Up in the Side-Galleries

Once they were adventurers who dared
to come in search of the glittering fruits of the earth.

Now the most they can do is tumble apart
to frighten girls in crotch-hugging dun-coloured shorts.

God in Heaven, the way their jaws clack open!
The way they offer bone's best to the mirage of flesh!

Individual Culture

I

The oven gloves were not to hand,
so I picked up the kettle
with a pink sponge rabbit, which was.

II

The rain arranges round every oak tree's bole
splashes like the gaping mouths of nestlings.

III

You tried to get your favourite private word
admitted into the Oxford English Dictionary,
but they weren't having any,
and so you continue to *lobble* only with friends.

IV

If wine were blue there would be no need
to describe this singular sky.

V

Above the faceless heads of the crowd
a tuba seems to be gulping light from the snow,
trying to rid its mouth of the taste of warplanes.

Common Property

I'm lying of course
but I once had a morse telegraphist friend
who told me how startled he'd been one rainy evening
to hear the upturned bucket in his yard
instruct him quaintly to go and eat his mother.

I revealed in return how obsessed I'd become
with the notion of raindrops falling inside the chimney,
adding to thousands of feet through clandestine air
another thirty through the centre of my house.

The Seventeenth of June

(for Ken Steedman)

Back at tea-time. And a lace-wing inside the house.
Lovely *Chrysopa*, on a towel smelling of rain.
Which shews patience enough to bask a while in our joy
(at its having been rescued from death by folding up)
then disappears at speed about its business.
I think I will thank Saint Briavel for this,
whose day it is,
and about whose life nothing, whatsoever, is known.

I encountered a fellow pluviophile earlier on.
The sudden secret handshake of our talk
I must confess has cheered me up no end.
There it incredibly was,
the telling me how in weather akin to this,
his wife would opine him crazy,
his fancy to sleep among lumber in the shed.
Pass friend; and when you cease to exist
go straight to Heaven, up through a summer downpour,
but keeping dry all the while, as if there had never
been other ways to travel.

The day recounts itself backwards.
At the bus stop this morning
I was thinking how simple it sometimes actually is
just to set things in motion,
to do as we've every One been done by, in fact.
I hoped that when the evening finally came, as it has,
I might find some words about English coastal parishes,
each with its beacon, spire, gallows,
ragstone tower or en-hillocked elm as landfall,
to be battered towards by crumster, cog and barque
through stillicidous arras or wrist-wraithing bone-racking sea-roke.
And here they are.

I wasn't quite sure what I wanted them for at the time
but now, in this silence, I bless their superfluity,
welling over the rounded rim of a day
of huge balneation, spargefaction wide,
the workings of grace made both pertinent and strange,
its conduits quick with all the sanctions of water.

Line with Atoll and Idol

As if were being drawn a thin black line
in the air a dozen feet above the sea.

As if it travelled parallel with Ocean,
but Ocean lay calm in an everywhere shallow bed,
devoid of ornament,
and never did wave snap hungrily up at the sky.

And as if that part of the line which moved
(for always these things are hard to comprehend)
made headway toward a coast,

but the bench of the island beach
sat nearly a dozen yards above the water,

and the line in its blackness was halted.

And as if, held in a nimbus of black sand,
the glassy basalt pillbox of the island
were nodding like a head from the eighteenth century,
which wore in accordance
with fashions not now understood by us,
two cloths as caps, the first argillaceous
                                        and the second a yellowing sward.

And centred on this atoll were sitting astride
the ridge-pole of her roof a Golden Woman,
who laughed, and cried, and sang, and through whom, waving,
expressed itself a continuum of frenzy;

and as if the thing most worthy to be noted
were how, if she'd only known that she existed,
she'd have ruled her *Realm Entire* from that vantage,
scanned the lagoon,
tasted the brassy sun as a serpent
lying coiled upon her shoulder,
and the rain in the wise of the forest's waxen cups;

and as if this were true, and All, and she marked from her chair
on its special swivelling mount
the four tracks which, when they met in the slits of her eyes,
had quartered the island between them, and made into a temple
her house through the doorless apertures of which,
in search of its earthen floor, the fowl from the woods
had all day strutted and pecked, and her eyes were not figments,
and the island more than smoke on the distant horizon,
and the thin black line which had travelled so far over Ocean
with its beach-head secure were now moving inland from the shore.

Cosmological

Spirals of brick-red gas.
Mind that broods
on the interstellar wind.
Sign of the Gnostic Heart of Jesus Christ,
creaking and swaying outside some deep-space tavern.

And here we stand.
Staring into the farthest reaches of cold.
A dog bays at the moon,
and that ever dutiful engine
hears and hurls the Holy Family's shadow
to be splintered against the earth,
to be thieves caught climbing among the star-blanched boulders
which strew our hillsides,
beneath the walls of our towns.

Staff Only

I'm drinking tea in a furniture store,
idly thinking of Phoebus, the sun-god,
when a sky-blue sofa on which a youth reclines
glides slowly through the cafeteria,
pulled by a couple of girls in nylon shop-coats.

I used to enjoy such theological problems
but now they make me tired, as one is tired by a child.

I watch in the last few minutes of my lunch-hour
this tableau as it steers its direct course
towards regions where no customer ever goes,
through swinging doors equipped with rubber aprons
which gasp behind it as it disappears from view.

Pokerwork

I fell in love with the vine-entangled cabin
in the instant of reading its charmingly different name.

The fact that I'd rented the only shack
on the whole damn mountain
that wasn't called *Cloudy Pines,*
White Smoke Table,
or *Iron Moon-Kettle Madly Boiling Over,*
didn't perturb me at all.

I knew as soon as I set down my bags at the gate
that if there was one kind of conversation
I certainly wouldn't be overhearing that summer
as friends made plans outside the General Store
while I purchased kerosene
in its cool, high-raftered and oatmeal-scented interior
it was this:

'How about taking some beer and climbing up
to *Bucket of Rusty Nuts and Bolts* this evening?
Watch the stars rise. Have us a *haiku* party.'

No. I think I can fairly claim that right from the start
I'd have wagered the end-most joint of one of my fingers,
to be severed against a boulder if I lost,
that this was not what the Boundless Void was proposing.

Not that I minded. As I say,
I loved my chalet from the moment I first saw
its cedarwood signboard,
the deeply scorched and somehow rococo calligraphy of which
inspired me with wonder, longing, and most deeply reverenced
presentiments of solitude.

An Office Memo

TO: *Julia*
FROM: *Brian*

When I got here first thing this morning
I discovered Gabriel, that trainee you sent us,
kneeling down as if composed for prayer
in front of my micro-computer.
I registered my surprise,
whereon he quite brusquely gave me to understand
how certain he was he could put it together again.
He called me 'Jack', and exhorted me not to panic.
I would probably not lose many, if any,
of my files. There were numerous yellow 'bobbin'
things lying beside him, carefully arranged
in the form of a Cross of Lorraine.
These he proposed to 'de-coke', I think he said,
with judiciously moistened twists of toilet paper.
I found his nonchalant, 'make-do-and-mend',
supremely proletarian kind of self-confidence
quite distasteful, and must have telegraphed as much,
for he stamped on my foot and proceeded to disappear.
I feel poorly, and am just about to go home.
The bobbins have begun to tick and smoke.
I thought I had better
get in touch with you about this.

The Tar on the Roads

Seventh day of the heat wave.
Buying fags after work I tried to remember
the last time the tar on the roads had melted.
She said with cars going past all afternoon
it had sounded as if it were raining.

There was quite a queue at the bus stop.
The man standing next to me said it needed a shelter.
Before the winter came.
I said I knew what a very grim place it was
to find oneself on a January evening.

When the bus arrived, I paid and went upstairs.
All one side was old people, coming back from the coast.
They looked really done in.
They sat alone on the outside of their seats,
and guarded the empty spaces next to them.
It meant I couldn't get myself by a window
on the left of the bus, as I like to,
and consequently had to sit down on the right.

I was faintly annoyed.
And desperately hot.
And rather keenly looking forward
to discussing the heat with my wife,
to telling her all about loudly hissing tar.
As far as I recall,
no one spoke in that upper saloon
during the whole half-hour of my journey.
I stared from my window.
I watched someone close a window against a draught.
I looked at the yellow fields of the valley floor,
and once I let myself glance across the aisle

at the faces of the pensioners,
but they seemed so tired and angry
that I chose not to do so again.

I was glad when the time came to walk.

The pavements were empty
and the melting road had been dusted with fine white gravel
so that everything looked like a postcard of nineteen-thirteen.

I was very hot indeed.

The worst thing I ever heard on that bus
came out of the mouth of a soldier going on leave
from the Army Transport School,
a mouth he was using to tell another squaddie
of what he'd always wanted to do to old women,
pointing one out down below as we crawled in the traffic,
walking beside us with some letters in her hand.

That was on a summer afternoon too,
one not as hot as this, and when I finally got in the house
the living room was like an oven, and my wife and I turned
each a gasping visage upon the other.
The television was going
and the newsreader was saying to several million people
that Highways Departments throughout the entire region
had been forced to grit the roads today to stop
the tar on them melting, except she didn't call it tar,
having had her orders to refer to it as bitumen.

He Loves to Go A-Wandering

Alone on an upland trail,
having left his wristwatch at home,
he takes a telescope out
and scans the surrounding hills.

What luck!
There's a long-case clock in a meadow of wind and herbs
with its face turned towards him,
and it's not as late as he thought.

He observes it long enough to make sure
that the minute hand *is* moving
then stows the glass
and continues on his way.

Later, towards evening,
with a limestone boulder serving as rustic desk,
he lays out notebook, bacon beer and pencil,
and memorialises thus:

The Lord is my Shepherd.
Special pockets all I hoped they would be.
Telescope splendid for telling time among mountains.

A Malediction

Spawn of a profligate hog.
May the hand of your self-abuse
be afflicted by a palsy.
May an Order in Council
deprive you of a testicle.
May your teeth be rubbed with turds
by a faceless thing from Grimsby.
May your past begin to remind you
of an ancient butter paper
found lying behind a fridge.
May the evil odour of an elderly male camel
fed since birth on buckets of egg mayonnaise
enter your garden and shrivel up all your plants.
May all reflective surfaces
henceforth teach you to shudder.
And may you thus be deprived
of the pleasures of walking by water.
And may you grow even fatter.
And may you, moreover, develop athlete's foot.
May your friends cease to excuse you,
your wife augment the thicket of horns on your brow,
and even your enemies weary of malediction.
May your girth already gross
embark on a final exponential increase.
And at the last may your body, in bursting,
make your name live for ever,
an unparalleled warning to children.

A Bee

Become at last a bee
I took myself naked to town,
with plastic sacks of yellow turmeric
taped to my wizened thighs.

I'd been buying it for weeks,
along with foods I no longer had a need for,
in small amounts from every corner grocer,
so as not to arouse their suspicion.

It was hard, running and buzzing,
doing the bee-dance. I ached
at the roots of my wings, and hardly yet discerned
that I flew towards reparation,
that in my beehood my healing had been commenced.

Words they use in this hive. To me it seems still
that clumps of tall blue flowers,
which smiled as they encroached,
had been born of my apian will,
in which to my shame I struggled for a moment,
and stained the air with clouds of my dearly bought gold.

Next

Next is a porcelain plaque,
fixed by a nail
to the trunk of a churchyard yew.
There's a supercilious pillock in a trenchcoat
standing next to it, holding a clipboard,
and talking straight to camera.
Yeah, right first time.
It wouldn't surprise me
if he's talking about that plaque,
but then again
his subject might be anything.
Putting him under the tree,
in its ravaged circle of acid litter and gloom,
might prove to have been a mistake, though,
for now the rain-cleansed afternoon country
which falls away in all directions behind him,
will come out wrongly exposed.
This may, of course, be the very effect they're after.
Or it may be they just don't care.
The plaque carried an inscription once,
a biblical reference
in black and heavily serifed Roman caps
which nowadays is eloquent only
of the sad effects of two hundred years of weather.
I love that kind of thing.
You can still read the name of the Book in question (*Judges*),
but chapter and verse have completely eroded away.

Jottings from Northern Minsters

I

limestone jazz

woodland clearing
with stiff-leaved clarinet

doorthud on airspace
where echoes fall into dust

for regimental colours
a row of smoking trombones

II

Cathedral Shadow
flits the length of the nave.

Squats on the altar rail
staring into the light.

I think he's recalling
his life as M.R. James.

I hear him implore me
to change him back to a sparrow.

III

Lightning at York,
to many in the Faith,
was a sure and certain sign of Divine displeasure
at the blasphemous enthronement
of Jenkins as Bishop of Durham.

I don't see it that way.

If God had really deployed Omnipotent Fire
it would doubtless have been for more amusing reasons,
perhaps to alleviate local unemployment
with a nicely considered Job Creation Scheme.

IV

The poet staggers down to the end of his garden.
Directs a stream of piss at a clump of bluebells.
Completely bloody useless.
He's wasting his time
with this stuff about cathedrals.
He gazes at his shoes.
And quite without warning
discovers the night transformed into *Oberon's Glade*.
He raises his head. Above the rooftops
a wind from the south has shoved some clouds aside
and the lunar chalice is spilling its silver light
through the delicate tracery
of his neighbour's mountain ash.
It takes a moment, then the poet starts to laugh.
A state of gleeful reverence sets in.
All the way back to the house he sniggers and nurtures
the penultimate grace of knowing he'll finish the poem.

An Expedition

Down to the end of the garden in the night.
With cigarette and glass of ice-cold milk.
I pick my way over heaps of builders' rubble.
Light from the new kitchen window comes along too.

Spade

(for Sarah)

Spade that wedges
the broken door of the hutch
and stops our rabbit
escaping into the night

Spade which denies to black rabbit
his leaping over the sage
his crouching in warm dark wind
his vanishing act until morning

Spade which gets handed
like a baton by moon to sun
and has been with me years, houses

Spade that but a moment ago
I imagined made out of glass

Sunday

(for Pat)

You start to wash the window,
find yourself peering out
at a foggy autumn morning.
Then you stop and smile.
Just can't tell
if you're getting it clean or not.
When you've gone
I sit and stare at the fence
where it joins the back of the house.

It's all I can see.
A sparrow lands on it,
but only for a moment –
the length of time it takes
to leave it empty again.

Elegiac Alternatives

I

Along the hull of an unladen barge,
riding high in the yellow afternoon,
the river casts reflections that resemble
the distant wingspans of ocean-going birds,
glimpsed at the moment of their sudden coalescence
into one great pensive Form,
beating low above shining level waters,
in certain flight towards an unseen coast.

II

Rabbits graze the edge of a cornfield at dusk.
A wicker bath-chair hangs in the top of a tree,
the roots of which hang over the edge of a chalk-pit,
its floor already in shadow. Another night begins.
Flame goes aloft in the rigging of the thorn
to view the sun as it sinks below the hill.
In the aftermath of an almost forgotten explosion
unspent appetite poses a moment as silence.

Chandlery

Here is your wooden keg.

It contains your astrolabe,
carefully packed in oysters.

I could do you black powder
if you cared to change your mind.

Or from perfect darkness a tethered animal,
one that would give you some milk.

One Mile Wide

Way it gets dark here.
Down by the water
the sky turns out its pockets
and goes to sleep in the grass.
Five white stones next morning.
All night long the river singing of home
to stones which might
if things had not been different
have been stars.

THE CLASSICAL FARM

(1987)

...which is a most parkely ground and Romancy pleasant place:
heretofore all horrid and woody...

JOHN AUBREY

...the richness and extent of Yorkshire quite charmed me.
Oh! what quarries for working in Gothic!

HORACE WALPOLE

A Priest in the Sabbath Dawn Addresses His Somnolent Mistress

Wake up, my heart, get out of bed
and put your scarlet shirt back on and leave,
for Sunday is coming down the chimney
with its feet in little socks,
and I need a space in which to write my sermon.
Although the hour's already late
it can still be done, if only you'll depart!
Down the pipe and out across the lawn
would take you to the station yard
in which you left your bicycle last week
and give me time to clothe in flesh the text
I have in mind for the instruction of my flock.
Please hurry, dear. The earliest note of the matin bell
has left its tower like an urgent dove
and is beating its way to woods outside the town.
The sun is up, the parish breakfasted,
the ghosts are all returned into the flint
yet still you lie here, shaming me with sleep.
Wake up, I say, for Sabbath legs
are landing in the grate. Go naked if you must
but grant me these few minutes with my pen
to write of how I cut myself while shaving.
Be useful, at least, and fetch my very razor,
for the faithful have set their feet upon the road
and are hurrying here with claims on the kind of story
which I cannot fittingly make from your sudden grin.

By the Fire

It's quiet here.
I'm dozing by a quiet fire
on a December afternoon.
I'm lying under an old coat
for the cure of my soul.
A recorder tune comes floating in,
and *float* is a good word.
It's vernacular,
just as the tune is charitable.
We go back a long way. We are old,
and need not listen to anything less.
There's a blend of arrogance and compassion
I've long been trying to put my finger on.
I think it lies beneath an overcoat too,
and hears the hiss of the gas,
and vagrant playground tunes.
When I close my eyes
I can still observe this room,
my table, the books, a milk bottle.
A bed of coals is glowing and dancing
in a grate that was torn out years ago
and it doesn't even seem strange.
I'm lying between two fires
in the quiet they've sometimes afforded me here.
I feel their warmth, and look –
my eyes are closed.

Truants

How long is it
since we fled across the fields?
We can't remember.
We camp in this broken railway house
or sleep in shallow ditches.
Butter floats in our black tea,
and painted pebbles dangle in our hair.

We do remember our predecessors though.
One, half-crazed, stayed away for three whole days,
almost too dumb to feel the cold,
afraid of the blame for a borrowed pushbike.
In the end policemen pokered his friends
with operatic frighteners that elicited his den.
They trembled. We trembled. The Majesty of Law.
There was laughter in the staffroom later
but mostly I think we envied him
his fear and his conviction, his adventure.
He turns an original face upon us now.
All that loyalty, he says,
all those ketchup sandwiches they brought me there.

The Bell

The Europe of the heart,
and a bright wood there.
Listen to the bell.
The ears attend
the spasms of a yellow bell.
Breath from its old mouth
subdues the quilt of countries,
a blanket on a sickbed.
The squares of mustard and the squares of potato
crumple under the heat,
which ruts like dogs
on the uninspected roads.
The hot wall of twelve o'clock
pushes history west.
Barns go down. Fields and churches fall.
The land permits
a hard tide of trees.
It is eaten by roots.
The heel of a gnarled hand
forges and bakes,
ferments and brews.
Ponderous and momentary hands
have twisted rope in rope-walks
and cast a bell in sand.
Someone was lost once.
Someone still stands immured
inside cold masonry,
exercising sound.
In the Europe of the heart,
in a bright wood there.
The yellow is like the flat of a blade.
The heat is from a chill belfry,
moving west with the trees.

Anatolian Sequence

1

going there on a
long train
like I did waking once,
the slate-eyed syntax
of the border
the way the left hand
door its window
and swaying connections
elucidate the mountain

2

whose god has erected
two signs
one on wood against
trespassing
and one perhaps on stone,
bearing the name
'Lake Van' it seems
in its signifier as
bottomless and deep,
a delivery
of the deepest
parcels of water

3

which are posted into
the space between
a man and a child,
who doubts the whole
demeanour
of this country

but look
it is, it is surely
getting more Turkish
cubing itself on glass
and steadily, greyly
announcing its profession

A Winter's Fancy

> To write a *Tristram Shandy* or a *Sentimental Journey* there is no way but to be Sterne; and Sternes are not turned out in bakers' batches.

A winter's fancy.
I look out of my window
and perceive I am Laurence Sterne.
I am sitting in Shandy Hall.
It is raining.
I am inventing a Bag,
which will accommodate everything.
I'd weave it out of air if I could
but the rain slants down like a page of Greek
and the afternoon is a dish of mud,
far removed from gentle opinion.
I am heavy with God.
The weather used
to cloak itself in sentiment
but today it imitates the tongues of men
and wags in curtains at me, along a yard.
I am also John, an elderly bibliophile.
Once, long after I died, I returned to Coxwold
on a literary pilgrimage.

A red-faced lout leaned over my gate
and instructed me curtly to Sodding Sod Off.
He was full of choler.
I sometimes feel I can understand
what's been eluding me ever since Christmas.
I'm exhausting my karma of country parson
in a dozen lives of wit and kidneys,
caritas, the pox, and marbled endpapers.
Looking out from here, this afternoon,
I can just discern the porch of my church
where Nick and Numps are sheltering from
Thucydides, Books Six and Seven.
By the look of that cloud looming up like a skull
there will soon be nothing left to do
but to take to my bed.
The cattle squelch past beneath a sodden sky,
below my windows and before the eyes
of Peter Didsbury, in his 35th year.
I consider other inventions of mine,
which rise before me in the darkening pane.
Light me that candle, oh my clever hand,
for it is late, and I am admirably tired.

Traffic

A truck full of shingle
crawls past our window
on its way from the river

Its headlights are on

and it has the words
Ocean Derived Aggregates
printed on its side

I did not see this yellow truck
just heard you tell me of it

I was looking at the rain,
watching the water
bouncing off the pavement
and sluicing down the drains

Night Moves

> Workin' on mysteries, without any clues
>
> BOB SEGER

He got much younger and smaller.
Two police arrived and took him out of the bar.
The street received him as a child.
He broke away when he spied the fortunate bus.
I had to throw a handful of coins to him.
Shillings and dirhems clanged on the metal floor.
Our policemen frighten me a lot.
They weren't in any hurry anyway,
standing by the railings in the dark.
They still had hold of his friend.
Their car was parked in the side road
that leads to the Royal Infirmary.
The yellow doorway crawled along the kerb,
the kid in a jersey, the conductor with a moustache.
I stayed crouching for a long time
as if on a sunlit bowling green.
My open hand was filling with sodium glow.
The gaze of the police was like
the nearness of the pavement to my knees.
Night's inexplicable actions. These night moves.
The railings released the breath they'd been
holding on to all day.

The Smart Chair

I heard my own voice.
It came to me in a room and it sounded strange.
I didn't recognise it.
I didn't even know it had happened.
It was a dark voice. Or a very white one.
It was like your daughter when she said,
'Your chair looks smart,' and then grinned at me.
My chair looked smart because it had a tie hanging over the back.
She's eleven years old, and although she knows I don't wear ties
she didn't know I'd been to a funeral, wearing that tie
which now improves my furniture. I wish I was able
to tell you all the things that filled the last two days
and which of them relate to that voice that came to me.
The wind in the brown pines on Church Island might have done,
and my fear when that truck moved over on the motorway,
because I really heard it,
but trying to tell you might stop me finding out,
and I've had to forbid myself enough already.
Certain proper names are forbidden to me now
for I will not have them do my work for me,
which ought to be done with a simple correctness.
It is like your daughter saying that the chair looked smart.
Just to make it perfectly right she put a knot in my tie
so that it was really being worn by the chair,
looped around the top bar of the back
and not just draped over it. I thought she did it with panache.
I thought this when I got back tonight after two days' travelling,
for of course I hadn't noticed at the time, and then I went away.
I slept in a white room on a striped mattress,
with stains that were like the maps of skerries and small islands.
Slept in darkness, naturally, not yet knowing anything
of the brown pines on the real island
or the attendant rocks for pegging Holy Sinners out upon.

This was all by the bye and for the morrow at the time,
like the stripes on the mattress, since I went to bed in the dark,
or like the poems by Reverdy and Desnos I got shewn after breakfast,
before our walk, before we started driving back,
before the wind that freshened throughout the morning,
moving the flowering currants that grew among the graves
and saturating with fine colour the walls of the houses that lined the coast,
turning them all into poets' houses, the houses of poets,
in which talk about seagulls was under weigh
in voices that had sometimes come to them in rooms this far from home,
rooms with white walls that sailed in old and natural darkness,
sisterly to other rooms in distant houses
with chairs and random mental furniture,
all living the same kind of life as pine-cones, gulls,
a cathedral wind in brown pines, old urine,
and faces passing backwards and forwards
on a narrow causeway with shingle and lapping waters...
from which I remember that I saw
that a white farmhouse stood in the middle of the bay
on a rock that was little larger than itself. *Not* a farmhouse,
unless they farmed seaweeds, rats, and the voices of drowned sailors –
there wasn't enough room – but just a white house,
a casa blanca to go with the gulf stream palms
and the bay tree on the cemetery island, a whitewashed house,
as surprising as the reflection of part of the name Lloyd
carried unruffled by the wind on the back of a black tombstone,
a mirror for its neighbour and as unsurprising
as if a high-backed chair had reared up instead,
instead of a white farmhouse in the middle of the waters,
a sentient chair, a really smart one, dressed in a black tie.

In the Glass

Pegs left out on the washing line
Catch the light of the moon.
They present a savage necklace
Which the night is taking off.
I look out over small gardens,
Like my mistress.
I see myself reflected
In the glass at the end of the yard.

The Surgery

Rose red rubble constitutes the evening.
A man with a worn and shiny billhook.
The coloured marble forecourts
Of shops that vanished in wartime.

In the waiting room a young girl and I
Smile at each other, are nice and shy together.
I count all the things that had something to do
With this branchy evening in the future,
The thudding of children on the old linoleum floor.

The Smoke

i can still smell the smoke

abandoning the upper case
for the first time in years
i (a little i)
sit in bed with
bonfires in my hair

if this poem is rather short
or if it is like it is
it's because i'm very tired
and i did not write it till tomorrow

Death of Pan

The wax ran down the trees in Tuscany
for each tree was a candle
and turned into features as it ran
for the candles were hamadryads
(a kind of girl) that melted as if on pyres

At Vallombrosa
the most Chinese place in Europe
we climbed through the pine trees and the cloud
to find that Milton had been there before us,
an Englishman,
who never heard the word 'Tao'
though he'd stared into its cool and smouldering bowl

It's cold this morning and in the street
a scrawny female voice is heard, exclaiming
'the callous bugger'
to men who have been hammering nails in planks

The rowan is being stripped of its berries
from the top down, by starlings

The small still life on the chopping board
is nothing more than 'marvellous and empty',
a plastic flashlight half an onion
and a knife with its wooden handle bound in twine

Red Nights

The red industrial nights of summer
are typed on the back of a frightening letter,
one that will cause you an ongoing pain.
And tell you as little of the reasons why
as you'd expect from effete vernacular verses...
The word 'soul', somehow set down right next to you
on the back step, freshened by a little light rain;
the way the south face of the chimney stacks
collects the light from the roadway going north;
the weathered blue fence that froze all winter,
nothing less than happy in its literary colour.
There are ways of deportment under skies that mimic fire
which I hesitate to commend to you at this hour,
which itself is only a fiction –
allowing the dawn a sudden swelling cold,
chopping like huge waters under a riverside pier.

Home Town

Children and dead sailors lounge in salty parks
or lie parcelled in oilskins in boarded-up shops.
He strolls among them with a sword
or finds himself alone by a grey and angry sea.
There is much to terrify in this seaside town.
A striding man from a medicine show
treads on the middle air and scowls at him.
A wind machine blows scraps of alphabets
which burn about his ears. He steps into an upper room
and the floor is no floor, but an idle bed of dangerous machinery.
He could have perished in those engines,
or fallen right through the house.
How does he always rescue himself? He does not.
Surely one of these escapades would suffice to encompass his death?
It would, but something always rescues him.
Dark children offer him their hands in parks
that bob against the street like barges against a wharf.
The drowned recline on their elbows
and smile at a bureaucratic mistake.
Perilous climbs bring him out of the theatre
and the wheels that should have burst him open
never get further than starting to turn.
What is beginning to frighten him most is the rescue,
not the predicament. If the charred ideograms would turn to rain
he could believe in it, but they simply cease to blow.
The vaudeville morgues are not consumed in a flame,
he just leaves them behind him on a drizzling quay.
The hand that pulls him from the cogs and gears
is not attached to an Angel but only to the dark in the doorway.
He parks his ancient Austin Seven on a steeply shelving beach
and leaves the handbrake off, for it will not plunge
into the tall unconscious waters but simply wait,
between the ocean and the town. He crunches shingle,

and wags his sword at the flapping bones of a winter resort.
His car stands patiently, with her head between her wheels.

Mappa Mundi

(for Alan Livingstone)

In their great houses there were always tables laid,
piled high with simple food and books,
old tables that lay supportive beneath
a drift of nutshells and paper, sharp tools.
Returned from walking behind the byre,
or spreading lant from casks upon the fields,
it was at these boards that they received
the urgent message from the capital,
pushing cheese and almanacks aside
to unroll the hasty map, slopping a harsh red wine
into bowls, spilling it, augmenting the stains.
Later, brooding idly and alone
upon required action they might scan
the worn incisements of their tutored days,
the musical notes whose deep square holes
enlaced a fertile cartography,
in which each emblematic creature rose
above a smoking town, and called aloud
to the beasts at the corners of the world.
It was cold, and there was all of Europe
to decide, and Europe, hooded like a bird,
blinked in its eye-gapes and shifted on its perch.
It was ice. The ink in its beechwood wells
snapped to the black attention of winter,
while fields lay supine in communion clothes
waiting for the word, and a coney limped
to the doorstep of the hall for warmth,
or just to perish there. Tables, shifted nearer

to the blaze, supported the elbows of men
who watched themselves in dreams, in the gases
vapours and *language* of the hearth, for they
etymologised, and watched for others too.
Logs of poplar's yellow wood, the splintered larch,
fed a conflagration which all men scanned
to know their mind or find their visitors:
still many hours away, for example, a grandee in furs
alights from his carriage at a crossroad in the hills
and knows he is regarded, as he bends
to fill the carcass of a fowl with snow,
as well as who regards him. His clear gaze
is lifted for a moment towards a house
he travels to but cannot see, then falls,
as the eyes of his host have also fallen,
back from this fire to an erudite table,
a table spread with the things of the world
and cut out from the local forest years ago.

Talking to David

Blue smoke rises how I envy,
goes silently where?
The slide projector's on,
and all the bits are rising.
Bedroom window focuses late Phoebus,
hot on cheeks and hair,
and another term is always somehow needed.
Researching candour with which to de-school ourselves
we look at Jesus plucking pigeons from the clay,
but it is looking in mirrors.
We fly over waters fifty metres deep,
the moats that encircle castles in Northumbria.

Country Alembic

On this tobacco convenient road two crows.
It is Vineyard Street, and they know they perch in it.

O my twa corbies,
that which is swallowed in our recursive ginnel
is that which is excreted.

December and January
wet their beds in Vineyard Street, wet their beds.
Drink your cigarettes,
and look up the road to the castle.

It's the 1500s again.
The rain augments the brown flood.

You sit in the car rolling cardboard into
Pharos of Alexandria shapes.
You wind down a window
and blow through them, open eyed, at the birds.

Scenes from a Long Sleep

I

He thought the Moral Code
was a pamphlet obtainable
(price 1/6)
from His Majesty's Stationery Office

If he ever got hold of a copy
he would read Mr Hore-Belisha's Foreword
while eating pies and pasties
in the Curious Angel, Glidington

II

Cod and halibut basked on the waves
on the dark green Arctic main
One of them opened its fishy mouth
and delivered this quatrain

I can't go back to Greenland
They keep me out with an aluminium fence
It follows the coastline closely
I haven't used the Royal Bathroom since

III

He stood in the window of his auntie's house
and watched the Great Apes
who were just invading the town

They came on their long arms,
swinging from the eaves of houses
and casting naughty glances at him

If he'd known the words
feudal, *gable* and *marzipan*
he could have fostered their employment

Instead he just stood there in his dressing gown
wondering how a straight street
could be turned into such a crooked one

IV

The orchards outside the walls are hung with fruit,
squares of green and gold that swaddle the stone.
We are looking at maps, my sister, both ancient and modern,
and this is how it appears to us, the usage of the land.
What a distance they walked, those two Royal Persons,
when they made their circuit of Byzantium.
I see them moving in gowns, stepping amid flowers,
siblings who have this city as their centre,
its noise and its heat a haze on their dexter hand.
I see them stopping to pull down fruit, now he, now she,
or passing through trees to cross the great roads silently.
The city is full of their commerce but the suburbs are empty.
I do not think they talk much to each other,
or know if much talk is necessary.
The light and heat are from a sun in his splendour.
It is, and will continue, the middle of the day.

The Guitar

> And what if all of animated nature
> Be but organic Harps diversely framed,
> That tremble into thought...
>
> COLERIDGE

Aerial songs, estuarial poetry.
An electric guitar is being played.
Its neck is five miles long,
and forms a margin of the River Humber,
where the thin soils are.
Aeolus swoops down, and begins to bounce on it.
He has serpents in his eyes.
He plucks the strings
with his Nebuchadnezzar toenails.
He's composing a piece called Early Memorials.
A train comes. His pinions take him
half a mile high in a lift.
The train courses over
the frets of the guitar,
but it is going backwards,
towards the hole in the middle.
Coleridge is sitting at a window
with his back towards the engine.
He must have been lunching in Goole,
but now he's fallen asleep.
'Dutch River,' he murmurs, 'Dutch River.'
He's dreaming of the advent of the railways
but will not remember, because I intend to
keep it from him.
It's a mercy that is available to me.
The train steams through fields of bright chives,
then it reverses and comes back as a diesel.
A madman steps out of a cabin and salutes it.
He stands by the flagpole outside his summer *kraal.*

The engine-driver waves.
The engine-driver and the madman
both went to the same school as me.
They sport the red blazer and the nose.
They chat for a bit while the engine grazes
on the chives that spring up through the ballast.
'Nice bit of road,' one says. 'Aye, nice road,' says the other.
The sky is like an entry in The Oxford English Dictionary.
The earliest reference for it is 1764,
in Randall's *Semi-Virgilian Husbandry*.
The loco swings its head from side to side
with the movements of an old-fashioned camera,
or a caterpillar. The mythic god of the winds, however,
who is still aloft, is getting tired of attending.
He flies up the line and starts twisting on the pegs.
Lunatic, driver, and diesel all look up.
Their faces assume an almost communal rictus.
They all jump in the carriage with Coleridge,
as the mighty lexicon twangs. They wish they were asleep.
The god puts his face right up to the window
and shakes his horrid locks at them.
They stare at the cattle grazing in his fields.
They note the herbaceous stubble
which makes frightful his visage of mud.

The Jar

His in-trays are everywhere, like the mouths of Avernus.
This month, my prayers have all gone down
through that jar on the hearth, whose green glass wall
collects intransigent air, and tells tales
of the life of the Buddha. Why complain?
The world will either school me with desires
or guard me with the language of madness,
I am promised my death, and the rest will
take care of itself. In the meantime,
those buddleia spikes are nodding sagely
like lovely Asian women, and an ant traverses
a gypsy clothespeg, fallen in the grass.
Although I grieve that the discursive mode
is lost to me behind swords of conjoined fire
I take the roads that open to other music.
The anguish of a single human soul
may flow into the world's receptacles,
jars, boots, boats, words, hollow logs and
emptied bottles of mineral water,
and therefore I invoke them all for my
Ode to Broken Thoughts – like broken biscuits,
shaken in a tin on an open hand
to tantalise as if we were children,
while that master grocer in a brown shop-coat
who postures as my psychopomp
looms up in the smoke of his language and virtues,
moustache and teeth and famous leg,
with his fawning theft of the wisdom of mothers,
and his tales of once serving the monarch, or God.

Part of the Rubric

Write out the word 'picayunish' one thousand times. Make a solemn vow, never deliberately to discover its meaning. If the word is already known to you, ring British Rail on 0482 26033 and ask the price of a ticket to Edinburgh. If, knowing the word, you also live in Edinburgh, then go into the toilet with a hand-mirror and sit looking at yourself for precisely sixteen seconds. Write to me care of my publisher and confirm that you have followed these instructions. Please.

Eikon Basilike

(for the soul of William Cowper)

During the late and long continuing cold
I went for a walk in the empty heart of the city.
I stuffed the sun and moon in a deep string bag
and let them hang from my shoulder as I marched.
I noted the resemblance that my home now suddenly bore
to a level Baltic town, its frozen gardens, and its
bright green civic domes. The new white lawns
had frosted to such a depth that they'd lost
the visual texture of grass and begun to make pastiche
of a pavement, a complement to some old and
disgruntled buildings. I cast around for a route,
and chose to follow three hares in winter coats
who hopped across my path. They tempted me away
from that novel plaza which the ice revealed
and I found myself on a track beside a canal,
or rather a drain, which is different,
for it empties into the turbulent German Ocean.
There was dereliction on one side of the stream
and an Arctic kind of Xanadu on the other.
I shivered. My hip-flask was out of action.
I hadn't actually invented it yet
but knew I wouldn't be leaving it very much longer.
If this was what linguistic exercise meant
then I didn't think much of it. The deep structures
I could cope with, but the surface ones
were coming at me in Esperanto, and fragments of horrible Volapük.
I was walking through the urban fields that surrounded
the Stalag or temple or star-ship of the Power Station.
Yellow electricity vans kept cornering on the road
that crossed the bricky and entrenched landscape.
I recognised the faces of the drivers, and later spotted
most of the leading Romantic poets, all of whom were eating
substantial packing-up, in tents pegged out by the kerb.

It was a case of etcetera etcetera. Tiney, Puss and Bess
were proving considerate guides. I found I had plenty of time
to inspect the ceramic formers on their poles.
I noticed many ordinary things, several of which were lying
on the ice, between the high and weedy banks of the drain.
I began to think of the slicks of grey lawn that must exist
between runways on the edge of international airports.
Hot moonlit nights in Athens or Cairo, powdery channels of grass
that might just as well be anywhere, all of them rising in Hades.
The fat and impersonal transports were lifting on either side
and threatening my creatures with their cruel and silvery wings.
I could see the black pylons here and there but the power lines
were all of them lost in the low-level brume. I only heard them hum,
thrupping the atmospheric fridge with over and over again
a Vulgar Latin sentence which my guts were scarcely screwed to.
'It is all up with thee, thou hast already utterly perished.'
The hares bounded on, and finally halted outside the gate
on the bridge that carried the road across the stream
and into the precincts of the Generating Board.
I stood next to them, making the fourth in their row,
and I looked where they looked: below the rusty barbed wire
was an old white notice bearing the four bold letters
that denoted which mesmeric authority
we laboured under the caring aegis of.
Something – Something – G – B.
Like a name of God. But the letters were all wrong.
The three hares looked at me like animals in anthropomorphic films
when they've just led the hero to the scene of his triumph.
I thought I might begin to weep and yet I scarcely knew why.
The enamel plate was now announcing that this was *Eikon Basilike*,
a place whose sub-title I had no problem supplying
from my sad and emotional erudition, justified at last
by a portraicture of his sacred majestie, in his solitude and sufferings.

The Classical Farm

vetus ara multo fumat odore

HORACE, *Odes* III.18.

Flame in the evening windows of the school
has crumpled all the inside of the rooms.
Small fires smoke on every allotment below
but the source of the incandescence
is in the big red eyes of the Academy.
The kids have screwed hot sheets and planes of gas
to loosely fill the boxes of their absence,
have fuelled the massive antique stove of brick
beneath whose gaze the gardeners do their work.
An old man stands sagely folding polythene
and cuts it with a sharp blade from the east
which he reaches for without having to turn his head;
a golden bird aloft stands crowing into the cold,
and men who translate Horace in their sheds
are bending homewards, sniffing the air for rain.
All will come by wisdom on this spacious classical farm.
They stoop to pick up last year's brittle stalks
or clean a boot on a neighbour's crumbling fence.
They lean into the evening on their spades,
or calculate the autumns of each tenancy.
One has been here sixty years, a colonist
who wears his herbal fumes like cope and shawl,
another just a week, and both of them
are clearly to be reckoned in millennia.
The fertile grid behind me now includes
the altar, hearth, or small Vesuvius
of a cone I build and let the school ignite.
I am learning to know these fires, and have laid,
with funnel on top and a flue in its base to inspire,
my factory of ash for fattening small landscapes,
a working model of its great Platonic master.

The Pierhead

Slabs of water
slide on two rivers.
A dredger churns at the tide.
Its chains and hawser
make a brief stab at incandescence.
This is where
the Hull joins the Humber,
and the angle it draws
is just like the one on the map.
You can stand in it and gaze

at the last few teeth in a truly civic dentition, spaced along the bank. No radiance like here. Compounded of bricks and water by the afternoon, it walks through doorways and helps to polish hand-rails and counters, scour wooden floors. It could put a shine on bread. The sky has fooled with culinary metaphor. It's sharp salads in oil today, a classic, almost tasteless dressing

which drenches walls and cobblestones like rain. The name of the goddess of arts and trades is written on a board, painted in the livery of one of the old railway companies. The windows of the pub beneath it stare at the empty shore a mile away, at other windows, jugged with grey light. Mute and opposite hostelries wear faces like slices of meat, haslet for example, and wait for Byron to swim between them, for the ticket office is locked,

the last ferry has gone. A man sits perched on the roof of the covered pier. He's helping to dismantle it, cutting through the girders with a torch. A white flame springs from his wrists, and makes him look relaxed and critical, as if one more thing had been done in his honour. He sits on the throat that used to swallow cars and cyclists, rolls of lino, the wives and dogs of estuarial farms. The empty cross-section at the fluvial end used to fill with the side of the ship, the paddle reversing in its semi-circular house. Now it's just a frame to isolate some river with, an occasion to note the anguish of fast waters, and to guess at the speed and volume of their flow.

The News

At nine o'clock tonight,
crossing the road to the off licence,
protracted crumps of artillery.
Not thunder,
finally here after weeks of dry weather,
and not the Fleet, either,
which is still off South America.
Probably drums and canisters,
demolishing some factory on the other
side of the river; or poems,
or other unstable munitions,
going off in a dump up in Heaven, or wherever.

The Rain

Text and Exposition of a Northern Creation Fragment, for Neil Astley

I

It was cold and mythological.
It was coming sideways,
out of wide leather buckets.
The cow looked miserable too.
They was usin' Norwegian Hats,
to scoop some scary, travelling
gallons at her…

II

Lengwah oskoorah, como per stone-troll man.
Boskie, except no woulds or shoulds all that time,
but solarmente fake-its. Names like Linlithgow,
springin up like mushrooms, heavything in chaos
nd turnin into a cow. Spenz er time lickin
bark off this ole tree, she doo, likkin up Sol
n lettin it fizz on er tundra. Its Gertrude.
Bos by nomen Gertrude, meanin I of the day,
like Day's Eye, lickle yellow flower on lawns.
She have big sad rudes, roundels and mournful in them
all through the gert, and sumtimes by nighttime two.
It rains. As Dutchmen in their courage spraak
'Hit rayneth pijpestelen,' pipe-stems,
snapt clay rain with wholes þru the miggle,
witch brings us on to sound-change: deformed like miggle
R kekkle and bokkle, reseptickles for reign,
and manklepeace, but this need not be learned.
It is not in the Texas, and thus irreverent.
Sum phonemes diph-erunt in Niceland, esspeshly
for that old cow. Mudder milky and primal sacrud,
debutante in the larva feels all day
nd tryin to give berth to de world,
Adam nd Eve ploppin out de behine,

n muttrin in Shebrew, much as fallgoes:
Bearshit barrow elbow HIM,
ATE hash arm EYE him,
WE ATE all OUR ROOTS...
Nd as they mumble, their wordies tumble after,
big black let-us, like curly cow pats,
then claps of funder, mental fings
wot applord in the first drizmul doorning
of this nice planned-it Dehru. Lots of yellow.
All of them prattin about givin berf from their harmpicks etc.
Lots of fings sproutin in the shit and the butter,
a greenthyme beginnin ond þe brids layin eggs,
sky makin signs on the hide of wold Gertrude
and incest havin fun, like you can with six legs.
O noise! O-din! He oafens a Roger Casement
and show his crinkly cartoon smile. Dubbel ravings
are Disprin in his ears. They peck and bushel arownd his hed
like circumstandshall elegance, but dark. He pisses in his hat.
Udders will have yam for tea, or be *sic* in the bust,
but Gertie noo gats wazzed on by the god.
She fort he was upstairs, but parent-ly not.
It's coming at her sideways nd he's god all his frenzy with him.
Their faeces fill the side of the mounting, they luck as if
they're drunken lass at a nut-shy, they are like the hat,
they are fool of piss. Dilemma, waggin its horns.
Dingbat alone has the receptacle, the only deep chapeau
in the creole of asian yet, but wot about buckets?
Isseasy. When questings are arsed the gods will have the handswear.
The Dame has been droppin makars all this time, crawlin from every
nooky cranial, every horrorfiss. Poets and tanners,
nd tailors n perleasemen. *Flagrante,* her big mist-ache;
her Indus-tree and weird. It grieveth me, nd I try to look away.
A hat and buckets full of stale are blanchin-off the sky-signs.
I feel on her long tung the hot stale wot falls, I rôles her eyes,
but all the wile she is dropping trolls nd ice-men, she ignaws me.
She maketh boats of skin, nd pegs herself out for voidjiz

She watches her killdren and attentive to their stories.
They are droppin kin from their nosethrills.
The mounting is several leaks away and all the yewrine
is comin this long trod on purposefull. It is coald.
More than Oding and his crew have throne by now,
she is mudder of þe whirled, and drooping that cum-panio
which turneth round n piss on her. It is loaf-weird. The weed-feels wave
and her kids go shod in shoon. She sees them fool the land
and their spoking languish dairify like farms. The bride seas
thrill with fish. The herows make death and marridges
and their lifes are whide nd green. There are slave-chains,
nd dryin fish, and pelts of gests on doors, nd choppin invitin
necks off, and outhouses, and wind, and buried standin up
neaf de doorstone of de byre, like wotsisname, Hrapp – hauntin the garth
nd lookin up the shirties of the girls, lookin for mudders,
all the white flints of the post-hole in front of him
and the daily reign of the homecumin caddle,
blockin the light from the crax in the pavement,
steppin across him, and bathin his north face nd hair…

Old Farms

Old farms
swallowed by town
remain as gateposts
brick paths
and sheds.

I'm walking through the graveyard
thinking about them.
I note how splendid
the local silage is,
and spot a hairy
half a coconut.

It's Caliban, the little monkey,
peeping out of the grass.

This life of intimations
amuses me.
We come from the oldest farms of all,
and eat our thoughts like apricots.

Glimpsed Among Trees

The house comes on line.
Information that streams from its eyes like dots
seeks out a person who kneels on a brown allotment,
the month being March and the time of day noon,
the long spongy root of a plantain grasped in one hand
and the sudden wide notice of the house's attention
conveyed in open assiduous envelope, down to this plot.
There is no moisture anywhere. Friable skin,
untouched since Autumn last, denies it.
A dry sheet covers the lumpy mattress
that aches in the scarcely visited bedroom,
the outside tap has stained its rags with rust.
A cold as square as furniture, but white,
not I, not thou, despite the urgency,
is emptying the old tradition
of the high gabled forehead lost among trees
and leaving a continuum behind.
Nothing whatever to do with the 'arid soul',
for it is not didactic, it makes the mind go blink
with novel gravities. The boy's room, revealed
as if in his absence, to the cleaner, by his toys,
shows the broken bowl of an eighteenth-century clay
inverted as helm upon, and making to seem Mongolian,
the head of one of his metallic infantry. It snows.
His father the Doctor, demented by early hours,
leaves lemonade and cooking marsala
to go sticky in a glass, a tipple which
the blue-painted god of the morning absently retrieves
and carries with him to the topmost view in the house.
It is this broad prospect, and old 'intelligence',
which the kneeling man has knelt to cultivate,
and minutes spent replying to the sky
denote it well, the binary ons and offs sent back

up a still intact funicular to the roof, the line of the eye
engraved as in a diagram, Plate XXVIII for choice,
with barlets that pulse from a ball whose tender lids,
peeled back and gorgeous with lashes, will never blink
at that which is only physics, its trees relentlessly inverted
in air as thin as this and its cottages always held
behind hedges of optical glass, – it takes the petulant
volumes of lunchtime air to be libertine enough
to bring carelessness to empire, to bend that gull with fallacies,
or to plot the fog which will take the next day out,
a strike with a flannelled hammer to dispose
of sheds and cybernetic pastimes equally, which is what it does.
It turns the whole invective into neighbourly Walden Pond
with old and chimneyed Thoreaus standing round and hearkening
to the anserine cries in its reeds. It sinks the Marist Church
in a soup of such communion that its dedicated bell
can honour with one mouth the entire eroded coast.
Small flotillas hoot, the incoming geese give voice,
the larger cargoes stand in line off Spurn,
a white embankment indulges the Sabbath shore... It is the hour.
Noting the moon and the chains we are going to make our attempt.
We shall take this festering street and sail it home at last,
provisioned and coaled and silently observing
the estuarial forts as they slip by on the beam,
a drunken cry too close for the crew at the rail
and the Old Man biting his pipe and discerning,
'It is egregious, oftentimes. I lie in my bed
and wish I were mental, like Rawlings. I watch
the great timber of the plough, to which all the other
parts of the plough-tail are fixed, and I find that I am singing.
I say my prayers and do my certain sums. I like the number ten.
I am always counting on my fingers, or flexing my hidden toes
and I log those occurrences which I call my *Decades* daily.
Ten ivory beads in the form of geese breasting the air this morning,
ten sweet farts, ten persons of Belgian nationality, ten fascicles of tens.
I remember, once, I brushed against my sea-boots in the dark

and after I'd frightened myself incurred with growing joy
the thought of their emptiness as a witness to my work.
There are temples everywhere.' He ended,
and the problems of narration started up all over again.
That coathanger, hooked to the rusty guttering on the shed,
could not its suit of air be taken down and worn?
It is stitched with lights for the dance with the swart earth
and is only waiting for the dancer to come, whose coming was delayed.
Eighty years ago a girl out walking lost a button here
and it took down into the trench with it, sealed inside its glass,
the whole of the dusk which descended on the farm,
its fluting impermanent sounds, the language of the wildfowl on the drain,
the green and oily bulk of the engine, as it chained the evening
on its last and most festive traverse of the field. All this is known.
The button goes under the tap like a drunk, and its pitted face
is pinched between finger and thumb, and then pocketed.
Quartz from the lips of the tide shines like diamonds, then dies,
but this has been up and down in the earth, and has learned a thing.
Its stored reflections will always include the poles of the ferry at Hell,
its vibrations always be unwinding the band of the voice of the goose
as it beats from the drain to the dyke. I absolve you, oh my heart,
for you inhabit your vocative well, you have slept in old farms
and are watching the face in the glass, as Mr Lockwood did,
whose 'yell was not ideal'. Your only reader must absolve you,
for there is blood in your hand.
You have waked in the oaken closet of the day and found yourself
kneeling, the house overlooks you, and its phantoms regard you as real.

Cider Story

A daughter now for her blinded sire in England
Pronounces the Greek and Hebrew which she cannot understand,
Or carries him cider, along the whitewashed hall.

I hear her candid voice approaching, skirts on flagstones,
And it strikes me that, at twenty shillings a litre,
Cider is still, just about, affordable.

It is middle morning, one of those apple forenoons
Which make the fairest lineaments of England. I decide so
In my darkness, then return to my rigid black questions:

What kind of chair is this? Who released it from the native oak
With my person attached and set it down upon limestone?
The rhetorical pavement echoes the courteous step

Of my cool but resented dryad, who carries me cider,
Whose voice I detect in the apple-green light by the wall:
''Tis good for thee,' she comes trilling in consolation.
'And drink it up, now, that shall take thy mind off thy dole.'

A Shop

A small one in a seaport,
And a handful of semi-precious stones
Is rolling to a standstill
Along a cold tinned counter.
Light from the horn windows
Or which falls through greaseproof paper
Or which whispers words like 'oilcloth'
Reveals in the never-startled gloom
The simple evil of its sallow owner
To the slowly swaying, and dull,
And indifferent, customer,
Who pulls the drawstrings on the curious skin bag
From which this realm of scattered islands fell
And pockets it, idly watching the hand
That reaches for the heavy octavo ledger
And rests a moment on its massive iron clasp.
Irregular jewels stud that burnished sea,
Each garnet and carbuncle circumscribed
With three concentric lines, as on a map.
You are witnessing the typifying transaction
Of the commerce on a planet without redemption,
Where unredeemed adventures come to rest,
As somewhere they must, in the borrowed trappings
Of time and place, example and occasion:
A den near a harbour on a late afternoon
On a distant sphere where the fog and the bells
On the doors of the shops on the islands like dark gems
Conspire to evince a permanency of winter
I doubt if I am licensed to portray,
And which causes me to end these verses simply,
With what, when that large book is opened,
I pray it may contain, which is itself a prayer.

On the Green Phone

(for one whose Muse had departed, from another in the same predicament)

Ah yes, that emerald telephone
On which you ring me up to say
That the world of objects is empty.
Once it would have told you stories
On nights like this, but now it copies
The heart, and rings and then goes dead.

It's the same with me, old friend.
Some bastard somewhere with all the luck
Has written a poem which features a cloud,
A scarf, a lettuce, and Lithuania.
I confess because it isn't me
That I'm glad it wasn't you,

Allowing us both in charity to concede
All power to his elbow. As long, of course,
As it wasn't *him*. I couldn't stand it.
He wouldn't know his bum from *Locksley Hall*
Where *all* the rooms have derelict
Green handsets, and coils of bindweed

Are confusing the exchange. 'Don't worry, Boss',
We've been through this before – at first,
Each time a poem got laid to bed
Herself would throw a wobbly, if you recall,
And now, when our first books are published,
She's out the door again, her *Coriandre*

Corrosive in the wardrobe, and lipsticked insults
Drying on the glass. 'No need to fret',
But that's the point, you have to.
It's the scratching that shows the wound is healing
And at least when she left she didn't take
The inwit needed to describe the symptoms.

I once had a friend who, when he heard
Phones ring in unattended booths,
Would answer as the Indian High Commission,
Or God, or whatever took his fancy:
'I am the ghost of Howard's grandpa;
This is the voice of the lettuce you ate...'

It almost provides a model for both
The Muse and her subscribers, who
Are often on the line, occasionally answered,
But mostly observing the long hypnotic brrr
Of the dialling tone's unusable dimeters,
Or sometimes misled by a passing lunatic.

I've said enough. The hour is late
And the charges too prohibitive for us
Properly to pull these metaphors together.
Like you, I think, I apprehend the irony
Of kind remarks which assume that the girl
Is still in residence, or, even worse,

The unkind ones with which her recent absence
Would tempt me to concur. It's hard.
For myself, I'm putting my faith in history,
And the sudden fact that I tell you something
I dare not tell myself – 'She'll be back,
The green phone will ring again
And the furniture be swelled with fictions
Like the heart. Convince yourself of that.'

White

Waking at seven
to thick white fog

a candle still burning,
the stereo unit
still receiving power.

Window open –
good old boy,
for floating me in
and out all night,

not much birdsong
dark tree-shapes
one or two pigeons
pretending to be telephones

A Flyte of Fancy

When I die and arrive at the Pearly Gates
I shall doubtless discover
that Saint Peter is poorly and taking a few days off,
and that David Harsent has been booked in his saintly place,
who does not like my poetry.

Saint Peter would have asked me about rain,
knowing the thing I used to love behind all,
but David Harsent will insist upon discussing
pustules, catheters, feminine endings,
underpants and schizophrenia.

Among the things that make this poem a bad one,
and one that Harsent will be *entitled* to dislike,
is the specialised knowledge it assumes on the part of the reader.
The name of God's friend is known to the quick and the dead,
but who in the world has heard of David Harsent?

A Man of Letters Recalls an Incident in His Youth

I met him in the early morning hours.
I'd said goodbye to my girl and was walking
Back through the slanting streets to my lodgings.
He limped. A bullet wound. Small calibre.
And certainly the cloth was torn and stained.
He told me a story I could do nothing to but attend,
And must have asked directions to a hostel
For he ended up on my floor that night, though I
Recall that I offered my bed. Having me down as civil,
Privileged, I do not think he could understand
That third-floor room in impoverished Paradise Square:
The one-bar fire, the empty soup cans,
The ewer and basin composed on a marble slab,
The ridiculous chintzy chaise-longue. Neither could I.
He had a baffled interest in my dignity, but he was mute,
Reminded me of other toughs I'd met. One, in Soho,
Who wanted something with my name upon it
Before he'd cash a desperate cheque, was scandalised
When I showed him a summons from the Dean of my College.
Was that *good*, or had I been in trouble?
He needed something he could judge me by
Outside my presence, neutral, in his Blue Room, Adult, Cinema Club.
He sounded like my father; and I confess I have been pleased
With an interest that approximates to love to find
Most of these persons naïve beyond belief.
This one had quitted the City in the morning,
For his health, was going North with his story.
I seem to remember he would not accept any food,
No tomato soup, just a cup of coffee and an aspirin
Before he stretched his damaged leg to sleep. I lay in the dark,
While his snoring settled down into a rhythm
Acceptable to the alert piazza outside. Familiarities.
Night-birds cried in the slum of the rectory garden.

The switch on the meter revolved, the fire died with a clank.
A metal bucket beneath the laden desk
Waited for one or another young gentleman
To empty its contents over the landlord's bike,
Which stood chained to the apprehensive railings,
Directly under my window. I think I froze.
I began to consider my girl again, and then to writhe,
In a kind of pensiveness, stifling my rigid breath
With gulps, in case he would awake. What guest was this,
Who might be feigning sleep? I asked myself a question
That was answered by my shame. It didn't matter.
Just a criminal, who might rob or kill or disapprove of me.
A man whose story I half believed then forgot, and certainly one
Who would have a lot of pain from those stairs the next morning.

Long Distance

When last I called you up long distance
I thought the peculiar noises you made
Were caused by your sucking the flesh of crabs
From legs and claws in a dish by the phone,

Whereas what you were really doing, you told me,
And which I find just as pleasing to imagine,
Was licking Guinness-froth from your fingers,
Having just been out to buy yourself a bottle.

Events at the Poles

A metal shack in Antarctica,
home to several military personnel.
Another one like it near the North Pole,
this time full of meteorologists.
They look quite cosy, with their yellow arc-lamps,
their chimneys smoke away in concert
as if they both drew fire from Vulcan's caves.
All is silent. The equinox approaches.
Up to the door of each of the cabins
there trudges a postman, bearing an Easter egg.
The soldiers greet their caller gladly
and take him inside for a cup of cheerful soup.
The weathermen, though, who are all very surly,
can think of nothing else but the coming dawn.
They sign for the egg and send him on his way.
For some time afterwards his stumbling black dot
provides the major visible difference
between the two landscapes, then suddenly he's gone.
Nothing moves at the white ends of the earth
except two similar columns of rising smoke.
There's nothing to distinguish them for a minute,
but then a door like one on a furnace opens
and out steps a postman, turning his collar up.

The Hailstone

Standing under the greengrocer's awning
in the kind of rain we used to call a cloudburst,
getting home later with a single hailstone in my hair.
Ambition would have us die in thunderstorms
like Jung and Mahler. Five minutes now,
for all our sad and elemental loves.

A woman sheltering inside the shop
had a frightened dog,
which she didn't want us to touch.
It had something to do with class,
and the ownership of fear. Broken ceramic lightning
was ripping open the stitching in the sky.
The rain was 'siling' down,
the kind that comes bouncing back off the pavement,
heavy milk from the ancient skins
being poured through the primitive strainer.
Someone could have done us in flat colours,
formal and observant, all on one plane,
you and me outside and the grocer and the lady
behind the gunmetal glass, gazing out over our shoulders.
I can see the weave of the paper behind the smeared reflections,
some of the colour lifting as we started a sudden dash home.
We ran by the post office and I thought, 'It is all still true,
a wooden drawer is full of postal orders, it is raining,
mothers and children are standing in their windows,
I am running through the rain past a shop which sells wool,
you take home fruit and veg in bags of brown paper,
we are getting wet, it is raining.'
                                                  It was like being back
in the reign of George the Sixth, the kind of small town
which still lies stacked in the back of old storerooms in schools,
where plural roof and elf expect to get very wet

and the beasts deserve their nouns of congregation
as much as the postmistress, spinster, her title.
I imagine those boroughs as intimate with rain,
their ability to call on sentient functional downpours
for any picnic or trip to the German Butcher's
one sign of a usable language getting used,
make of this what you will. The rain has moved on,
and half a moon in a darkening blue sky
silvers the shrinking puddles in the road:
moon that emptied the post office and grocer's,
moon old kettle of rain and idiolect,
the moon the sump of the aproned pluvial towns,
cut moon as half a hailstone in the hair.

Eirenicon

These old blue boards
Were once a part of the fence.
Now they form a side
Of the much neglected compost heap.
They warrant a couple of lines
In a hopeless libretto of courtesy.
The night is full
Of such embarrassed recipients.
An iron pail,
Blanched in historical cement,
Mimics the cough of a child.
Simple poems,
In the gift of the summer,
Get shorter,
Deconstructing themselves.

The British Museum

We dream of the British Museum.
We want to return a winged stone lion
To the desert country it came from,
Outside of which it is dumb,
Outside of which a stranger to meaning.
The plaque that rests on its foot tells lies.
We know this script that decorates its flanks
And it does not mean what the keepers would assert.
They have built a vulgar café in an annexe
Which seems to feature sexual machines, vibrating beds,
For lunchtime liaisons we're supposed to think of as cultural,
But we won't. We're busy dreaming ourselves political.
An elegant system of sleep is constructing
A complex lodge for a free and scholarly people.
A state of grace that lies sleeping within the State
Is emptying its present halls of plunder.

The Globe

(for Leo Doyle)

Men are not gods. They just hold the same things in common.
Climbing the stairs to our bedrooms in the dark,
or idly gazing at landscapes from early albums,
crouched in a plastered outhouse of a summer evening
where it's cool and quiet and the light has failed,
we harvest the truth of those tentative statements
which were formed in the mouth of the bakelite wireless,
for its plummy plurals have continued to reach us
wherever we are in the house. Edifying Lectures at Dusk
float in and out of the windows like paper planes,
the kind whose bombload is held to resemble
the light reflected from jams in the pantry,
pear halves stacked in syrup in jars,
the breath of apples in the air raid shelter
and the sound of the clock in the hall that is ticking like fruit.
Please ask me nothing. A globe of inky but translucent glass
is slowly inventing itself, and turning into a sky.
The yellow panes of a window expand upon it and curve
like four birds flying away from a centre.
I stoop to look through them at mountain lawns
and a bent old child with a barrow on a path
who gradually straightens and shrinks, while I do so myself.
There are bird baths on Olympus, too.
Dressed in gas masks and a good deal shorter
we are playing French cricket next to one,
passing the bats around and around our legs
and eyeing the prizes of perfect fruit it supports
as if the centrifuge on the end of the arm
had just created loganberries and now sustained them.
The garden levels as I watch; the fence comes upright with a click;
a sigh from the bellows of an unseen camera –
and the outspread palm of the evening is holding up the house.
Here. Its bootscrapers stand in little religious alcoves

and vie with the kitchen drains in collecting the dark.
The bells in the bedrooms are stopped with paint
as fast as the mouths of the days of its servants.
A towel rail hums in the bathroom, a stirrup pump stares,
a medical dictionary sighs on its shelf,
and trolley bus tickets with different owners
flutter like moths in the back room we shared,
just glimpsed, as I open the door with love
to gaze at the absent inmates on the grass,
flying back to their piles on the dressing table,
and alighting in serial silence, like the days.

What Care We Shew

What care we shew, when we answer those who are sleeping.
Replying to questions about pits and burning towers
we utilise a grave and kindly voice.
Old heraldic hands, couped at the wrist,
clasp in the air beneath an ornate lintel.
The words are formed in different rooms of the dark.

The Barn

I stopped in the barn's wide entrance,
where the dust and chaff were like bees.
With the light behind me, and my rake across my shoulder,
I knew I resembled the Harvest as often portrayed.

'Bees' is what we used to call
all kinds of insects then,
and bees were in my mind as I crossed
the floor to where he'd fallen.

I'd never known him dead before
and therefore did not see him straightaway
but thought he was a sack,
with a barrow standing nearby ready to move him.

And move him I did,
though first I stood on that earthen floor
for a hundred years, while the language changed around me.
Dust. Chaff. The names of common things.
My hand moving up to touch my tightening cheeks,
to pick the pieces of broken bees from them.

The Fly

(for Ian Curtis)

Legs finer than this hair that just fell
it alights on my block of white paper.
I was going to write something down
but now I must pause to watch it work its feelers.

If even the otter is more different than it seemed,
'reacting simply to the sound of running water',
carefully plastering cruel loudspeakers
with sticks and mud, what can I say of this fly?

It has legs. It has antennae. It will have a triple-
jointed Latin name. Trying to get a pupil once
to describe inventively an inhabitant of Mars
I broached the subject of its sense-perceptors.

I wanted him to imagine a better way
of eating than punching a futuristic machine,
don't ask me why, was hoping he'd require
that it gulp phlogiston with its cerebral limbs,

extract subtility, or at least employ them
to carry its clearly audacious food
to the mouth on the top of its head. Blank stares.
The dutiful teacher must sometimes be content

to consolidate vocabulary. 'Look,' I said,
and put the backs of my wrists to my brow,
like a Spanish child playing bulls. 'What are these?'
And waved my fingers around, intent on eliciting

the strange questing life of our benevolent alien,
the skipping ropes that started from out the dome
which housed his spirit and his intellect. *Ex ducere.*
By art I would 'draw out' that which he did not

know he knew, something known before to which
he'd give the word, and justify my salary. 'Quick.
Come on now.' He looked at me as I just looked
at that fly which landed on my empty paper

and lovely recognition dawned, with all its expertise.
He put his fingers to his temples, waved them round,
and snatched his hesitant answer from the air:
'My Martian, when he eats,' he said,
could use his, you know, testicles.'

Vesperal

spiders, lately,
warm dry days,
and spiders everywhere

we'd probably call this
'spider autumn'
if we kept that kind of calendar

tonight you brought one down in a shoebox
and I put it outside
and then just sat and listened to the house

faint airs moving
across the mouth of the chimney,
our old white fridge
turning on and off in the dark

The Mountain Hare

(for Mike Boyd)

A white mountain hare
sits quietly on a stool
and watches the curatorial evening
fall through a bottle of wine.

Stuffed in 1926, you know
it has nothing left to fear,
has nothing to do but embody the silence
and share the light from the river with the walls.

It tends to be like that in this Museum,
and since such events are hardly other than real
the hare has decreed that henceforth they'll be known,
for simplicity, as December Afternoon.

Everything here, says the mountain hare,
resolves itself into aspects of collection:
while careless tides ascend the nearby staithes
some Sky drops in, to take a look at our bones.

The Northlands

No rain. No storm or thunder,
not even on the wireless. No lightning,
no rain.

But I'd been watching the lightning!
Either bounced off local cloud
or reflected in lucid mesmeric radio
from over the horizon
three whole days now,
which nobody else had,
and for three whole days I'd
thought I had epilepsy.

Not until I heard some tune
I hadn't been listening to
and which didn't impress me
was a Chopin nocturne
and saw how it and the night sustained each other
like two old con men telling each other tales
did I actually get the point,
and the intimate cruelty,
of the day's imitations:

a casual spread of laundry in the bath – Ophelia;
creased and mottled leaves from Summer
on Susan's Miss Moffat cap – the cunning Butterfly;
myself with fountain pen in hand,
- ah how much better than history.

Which is why
I'm confessing from here it was from here the first time round
that the lies *really* began and I began to imagine
the hills with all their electrics stilled

and *cattle pinned out like photofits in the glare*
and *my house that laughed in a curtain of rain*
but didn't embarrass me, though it should have done,
and even…
if I'd died that night how it wouldn't have meant
quitting this kingdom of metaphor
but leaping off the body fag in hand
to be some new kind of god for the northlands,
the *northlands,*
which actually frighten me,
which far from being a place
are a set of sounds whose transcription I think
it would be unwise to leave unrepented for very long,
whose transcription thank God
I think I am *unable*
to leave unrepented very long.

The Sleepers

They lie on short grass,
in a place where whiteness
builds hedges to filter the blue,
nowhere more than a dozen yards away.

Time eludes them.
Passing clouds have stained their backs
with unfelt shadow,
but otherwise nothing has moved.

Their small enclosure is the perfect frame
for all that a lengthy posture can express
of love or of strangeness,
two hands of cards disposed by careful hands
face down upon the turf,
as if in the expectation of return.

Hare's Run

Hare ran on mountain,
disclosed the boundless accidental
graces of his running.

What he did was go on up at speed,
consuming the functions of visibility.

He went in flame,
with feet of flame went utterly beyond.

A circular town of grey volcanic stone
when hare had passed it
unfolded into a bright assembly
the petals of its story,
its doorways and herds on an incandescent wind
were drawn by hare up the mountain.

For as fast as hare but always just behind him
his curious consort stepped
and glanced into caves where practitioners of breath
returned his stare from sudden columns of ash.

And still hare travelled upward,
and sprang across the tightest of the lawns
until the leprous slabs asleep on the summit
which now will bear his clover prints for ever
allowed him to lift through the towering stacks
of charcoaled birds his final narrative form.

Hare vanished then.
His shadow raged an hour among the rocks
and then went cold and died.
Of the thousand stories about him now in fashion
there are those which make urgent claims on hare's behalf
and those which simply invite the listener to tremble.
A while after hare had made his run on the mountain
a hissing rain commenced.
A few of God's more willed and habitual stars
arose unseen behind hare-shaped windows in Heaven.

Gillan Spring

What I'm about to write
has a necessary premiss:
I'm lying on the ground
in a kind of ancient encampment,
scrubby clearing, skin tents, stockade of thorns.
I can't raise my head for some reason,
perhaps because I'm pegged out with drying thongs,
so most of what I see and can report
is feet, sometimes bare and sometimes shod,
in bark or hide, is legs and the
clothing of legs, wound round with strips
or lost in the circular weight of a turning skirt.
The people here seem gentle enough,
so perhaps there is rather a wall of hanging vapour
which only leaves a yard of transparent air
like the breathable space near the floor in a burning house
and I'm lying down to feed my eyes in it.
Maybe it's the curtain of time,
which is usually taken to be vertical
but might well be horizontal, a blanket really,
and the wind has lifted it up for me to look.
However this is, there are certain things I can see
it would be wasteful of me not to try and relate,
the feet I've mentioned, but also the contours
of the bases of various heaps of equipment and
material, the fan of smallest bones
that have fallen from that large bleached stockpile
or the butts of the lances of ash
arranged in their careful tripods near each lodge.
Much of what I said earlier is extrapolated from this
and some of it calls on the language of geometry,
like the trapezium made by two legs planted apart
and crossed by the parallel lines of the ground and the fog.

It is through these early windows, so to speak,
that I gain my largest fragments of the camp,
the way the land drops away to the south through the scrub
and the sheen of distant water, mesmerised with birds.
There are poignant moments too. A stream of urine
arcs down from a hand that grasps its fleshy tube
and one of their small women, squatting to piss,
looks directly at me, with the only eyes I have seen,
for the body that crumpled fell with its face in the earth
and the most of the business has taken legs for its text.
It is as if I am at leisure, prone in the door of a tent.
My cheek collects the spattering drops of spring,
or there is sunshine, which is beauty, or snow,
which is a beauteous darkening, the way that wood
and skin and bone go black in a world of two colours,
when the working floors are covered and the wisest
people die. There is necessary laughter.
To some things, though, I cannot ascribe a season;
the doors of blood are perennial. Between two pairs of legs
that move a shouldered pole across my screen
depends the head of a stag going backwards,
its throat wide open and its antlers inscribing the dust.
With her feet in the hand of a boy, for I see him
as far as his chest, a swan prolongs her crimson neck
between two ruined fires, and a third
which it seems is never extinguished, for its hearthstones
are blackened with eld, and its topmost flames
are necessarily lost. Art, I am told,
concerns itself with the difficult and the good,
and this I'm inclined to believe. Not far from here,
no more than twenty minutes away by car,
is a field I first discovered in mid-winter,
its fringe of trees and scrub, its ponds,
and its permanent spring of clear matutinal water.

The Best Translations

A man invited a demon into his house.
That is the whole of a fairy story,
the familiar kind of popular horror
which lies below each classical literature.

The tale is made of an upstairs room
a civil square a casement and her shoes.
The best translations are those which had him
flee the temple in anachronistic clothes.

A Monastery in Georgia

after an account by Alexander Elchaninov

He climbs all day to get there,
ravine going down on his left.
Two stone towers,
two black 'beards',
water a mile away.

The bread is mildewed. They eat it in
the sunlight that visits the terrace.
The young one hems his robe,
the old one limps.
He was thrown from the wall last winter
by bandits who gained entry and found Nothing.

Twin towers. Two black beards
which wrestle with the liturgy.
He sleeps under sheepskins in his cell.
He walks in the pines and meets two men.
He only has two words of their language.

The nights are memorable.
The window embrasure is empty
except for the cold spring lights of the town,
where his mother sits, and his sister plays the piano,
where his hands rinse photographic plates
beneath the moonlit tap in the kitchen. He turns.

He snuffs the Georgian sky and then the candle.
The icon goes out, and I take my pen
and borrow his simple story of long ago.

Men have lived. Even so far from us
in place and time as this. John and Gregory.
I speak their names. I record my joy
that I did not have to invent them.

The Restoration

Birthday candles, strewn like the spokes
of sadly dismantled wheels,
could be screened going backwards,
could be seen to go back on the cake.

And brutal clowns, from their half-way down the lane,
could by invisible hawsers be recalled
to mend the innocent carts the very
sight of which had caused them to go berserk.

There could be restored, in the cinemas of time,
the luminous frames we imagine preceded the action,
even from splinters of wood and ruined foods,
the many morsels of glistening bright *gâteaux*.

THE BUTCHERS OF HULL

(1982)

To what shall the mind turn for that with which to rehabilitate our thought and our lives? To the word, a meaning hardly distinguishable from that of place, in whose great virtuous and at present little realised potency we hereby manifest our belief.

WILLIAM CARLOS WILLIAMS

I recommend the reader to examine carefully the face that is drawn on the shell of the crab.

AUGUST STRINDBERG

That Way Inclined

There's a gale tonight.
It's cold and I've got a cold.
I don't feel good.

I have Elastoplast on my watch strap
and wear an old jersey.

Perhaps I could turn Quaker
or seek out, in Tunisia,
a City, with flags everywhere.

Hermetics

The old man's letters
are word perfect.
Like weather reports, you said.

Traffic,
birdsong,
the windows:
tea here is always pleasant.

With more than one world
it might be easier.
I could watch us from the others.

In at least one way
this spring sun
is eating out my spine.

The Pub Yard at Skidby

Back of the pub yard the village
gulps downhill into butter country.
The gulch of cow parsley and marvellous docks
is a place where the sun has always westered
and I say I think I drink here
on the borders of somewhere 'very large'.
If there are holes in the sky
then this spins directly under one of them.
Significance floods in, and someone
is 'doing up a caravan' in it now.
To get those pagan discs and clusters right
(the hedgehog singing against the silver)
has taken him a year – and all his knowledge,
and all his lies. Just like it did theirs.
Up to our chests in the evening we for our part
have filched the eyes and hearts of faithful creatures.
Dogs, maybe, or bulls. How could we otherwise?

The Experts

A man who knows everything about pigeons
is talking to a man who thinks he's a Roman.
They are fishing the waters of the Kennet,
a stream that rises in the Marlborough Downs.
Their spinners with three hooks are meant for large perch
but what they come up with is chunky tesserae,
the ruined remains of an inundated pavement.
Few are the pleasures that can compare
with those afforded by a Berkshire July.

Everything has a Latin name
or speaks with the hollow mouth of history,
sits in a stand of trees and calls to you
or drags you under ground and breaks your bones.
At the next peg downstream their hirsute neighbour
has left his rod in its rest and is having lunch.
Holly leaves in lard in a rich bronze pan
punctuate the noontide with their distinctive crackle
and a rainbow left by the recent showers
bends into the woods on the opposite bank.
It was hereabouts that a blacksmith once heard
a prolonged and derisive burst of cheering
that kept him sober ever afterwards,
at home with his wife and more careful of
his forge and the custom of his native shire.
'In Gervase Markham's *Farewell to Husbandry,*'
runs the cheerful banter along the bank,
'there are ox-shoes with fullered grooves and calkins,
and drag rakes and heel rakes with split willow handles.'
They take their meridian ease, these labouring men,
as experts in the field have always done.
Lying on their elbows and beneath the open sky
they ponder the stolen grass, the common stream,
break bread and cheese and eat their eccentric meats,
and as the thirsty ground dries out again
flex their muscles a bit, fall to bickering,
throw chips of twig and ancient dung around,
then belch, fall silent, and finally fall asleep.

Celebrations

They keep on happening.
Through birdsong
Or a hot white road,
Sheeptracks, or the mysterious government
Of the blue sky at noon.
The rain can contain them,
Or whatever is lush –
They make abandoned holdings fertile,
And are often to be found
Alongside the derelict.

One day,
Perhaps I shall learn
To put a name
To these celebrations.

During a Storm

I'm the cause of all this. Of all I see.
In trays in every window
my seedlings scan the radio-source
like infant radar.
Seed-leaves sweep for thunder. Sweep my heart.
I manufacture sperm in weather like this
and expect my plantings to mimic me.
Explosive devices of dung quietly prime, and start to tick.
The lunacy of the transparent bird-scarers
goes 'coptering up to a scream.
The slugs no longer require
upwards of two days to die
but glide and curve like tracer,
lighting the wet paths.
I should get a grant for this establishment.
I can't afford the dishes and masts
which would symbolise my real intent here.
I'd rather have stood in the doorway and watched the storm
but I lost control of the metaphor.
The gulls coming over with breasts like bombers
are my responsibility.
I tremble at the crisp commands I make.
I watch myself move to escalate a war.

Running

It grew lighter as the afternoon wore on. The sky blanched, and curdled, and grew big-bellied; but it meant nothing to the man. Once, about the fourth hour, he startled a plantation into blue and gold. And later, towards evening, he skirted the corner of a field, away from a line of thin shaking men. When darkness fell, he was still running, but it meant nothing to him. Behind were the centuries of birch, and frozen bracken. Ahead, an untold acreage of beet, and the lean root fires. It was cold. The man moved inside a brilliant coldness, and watched the stars as he ran. The moon was dark; but the stars were like the hearts of birds, on fixed and acceptable journeyings.

Building the Titanic

The streets are full of air.
You quit the shipyard on the lunchtime shift
and we catch you there.
The gates finish opening and already our hands reach back
to empty *your* hands, your faces.
We work a black change on you.
Resolved into coats and moustaches
you are free, now, to consort like wolves on the snow.
We turn you into a thousand German orchestras.
You'd play for a thousand years
if we'd half a mind to ask it of you,
and we might have. We do all this
simply to hear ourselves say, 'This is what we know.
This is the lunchtime shift and even the trams are hungry.
They advertise bread. They will eat you, if you won't make way.'

Geography

The Caribbean has many harbours
black people bathe there

In China, they used to blow
up children's noses

Among Tibetans Schadenfreude is still widespread
though hardly ever meant

The Danube flows down to the sea
flirting a little with the gay young nobles

Back of the House

Sick of England, but happy in your garden
this hot afternoon, your English garden,
where everything looks like something else
and Language, fat and prone beneath her fountain,
idly dispenses curling parchment notes,
her coveted, worthless, licences to imitate.
There is too much to photograph here,
so put your camera down. Relax.
A fan of green depends from twigs like vines
but the punkah wallah has gone to stand
in the shade, where you cannot pick him out,
and grins at the print he left behind,
which moves its arm in air, and grins at *him*.
So pull the rope on the broken swing, to make us cool.
Impersonate a dancer from Bali or Siam,
or somewhere they posture with sticks and bits of string.
Look around you. That large bird was running away
from a poem by Keats, and it failed.
A pile of brushwood makes flagrant promises
to Andrew Marvell, and the boulevards are ringed by bombs.
Light, and shade, are the lustrations of *trompe l'oeil*,
itself the name of a garden in France,
and the three bleached poles that limit the brassica
make a hitching rail for goblin cavalry
in the childhood garden that continued to grow,
commensurate with our stature. 'How far we used
to travel in only three paces,' you say
as we take an unhurried dozen to the gate.
When I walk off down the hot brick lane
I know I leave myself behind
in the coloured window, in the Byzantine
back of the house. I watch us still examining
the blasted elm, that rocks to your fingers

and threatens to fall. It would lie across
half the garden. I estimate its height
and step that far away, before I go.

Three Lakes by Humber

1

Bright green:
silent stock-car 33
lies rotting in its acid

2

Recreational:
but a conspirators' canal dug overnight
to link it with its neighbour
would melt the pert clubhouse
and have its boats and water-skiers
floating belly up by weekend

3

Clean, and left to please itself.
two swans circling
on an Iron Age mirror

Strange Ubiquitous History

What age the world had when the trees took fright
we reckon and reckon and reckon it a recent thing
which was witnessed by our fathers
                                                            our fathers likewise
convinced that once 'the trees' had walked the earth
looked in lost valleys for the forms of last days
like tumbled down slopes or bracing themselves
or braking at the tops of slopes
or skidding arresting rooted
                                                    we are like our fathers
the trees all have smoothnesses
smooth enough to put faces on
startled faces formed when something
appeared in their sky and startled them
they froze like mice under a kestrel sky
like rabbits in the grass until it passed over
                                                                        just like our fathers
we're convinced it did not pass over
that something hangs in the trees' sky still
or that the generations of trees
bend and balance and grow into directions
because their fathers shout on the wind
we are still waiting the sky will clear
what age the world had when we first took fright
we can only reckon but reckon it a recent thing
which was witnessed by our fathers

The Butchers of Hull

The butchers of Hull, that summer day, did more than they knew.
Their lock-up shops were like Catholic shrines, like Walsingham.
I stopped on their streaming forecourts, all across the town.
I read their 'beast heart', and felt my own heart fill.

Upstairs

A motor owner,
you do not usually
travel this high.
You say you are surprised
by what lies behind walls,
by allotments for example,
and their networks of decay.
Your surprise surprises me.
You should learn to look
elsewhere in cities.
Behind that main street yesterday
there were swans,
on the newly cleared drain.

The Specialist Heart

My inside pocket is my specialist heart.
I feeds it with papers.
We have filed our jackets with regularity
my fathers and I,
we make wardrobes into libraries.
Letterheads bills and annotated bootlace-papers
are our bones and our memories:
we write in indelible.
Our pockets swell to the old afflatus
of a war against women:
hushed tones, and angry glances.
Once a year, on Mischief Night
we frighten ourselves on the old stories
of female victories: jackets gone to jumble
and vanished patrimonies.
The pocketsful which made us stoop
to beauty or degradations
lie bundled by marriages.
My dads and I put in and in
for rust and moth
to work into treasuries.
The paper folds and un-folds
to make the cross that eats the paper.
We do a lot of unfolding, then.
We have learned to put in and in
to have our histories,
to build archivists' hearts.
It becomes a racial tradition
in the recent generations.
The discipline has settled
into generous options.
We know when to kill ourselves now,
how not to end up stinking of tobacco.

The Summer Courts

Written in the cells on a summer midnight.
There are six of them and mine is cool and bare.
They lie squared out a long way down beneath the courtrooms of the day.
Up there the sun fries our faces to match the city furniture
so we all look forward to the scented evenings.
The doors are opened at five and the cooling heat flows in.
Bananas and petrol and lime leafed avenues.
We smile at each other. Until tomorrow then.
I linger on in Court Number 5. It changes as it cools.
Or I watch the public gossiping on the steps.
Sometimes I match my descent downstairs
to the declination of the evening.
I am entirely alone in the building nowadays.
My wife has got used to this lengthening trial
and has been going home since April.
We make our affectionate until tomorrow thens.
She steps apart from her contending man.
She used to stay here but our sleep was fitful
and since April she has been clocking off with the guards and counsel.
Martinson the usher lives on her bus route
so at least she has someone to travel with.
I think he takes her to legal bars.
I like being alone in the building. And I am.
Except for the sentient public fountains.
I am trusted with the keys. They pay my wife
a small consideration for my role as caretaker.
I sometimes cajole the mice to play elsewhere
but really I do very little. I have access to the Constables' Kitchen
where I can make myself a cooling drink if that is what I want.
I have when I felt the need done handstands on the block outside
but mostly I stroll in the friendly moonlit corridors.
I've had to work for this. At first
I spent my nights subverting witnesses.

Being briefed by all my mythological characters.
They continually failed me. I failed to subpoena even one
who'd been dead long enough to speak with authority.
Not one had the eloquence to conclude my case for me.
McCool and Jonah and Lazarus
were courteous of course. They didn't seem to blame me
for interrupting their lunatic voyages
but they were simpletons. Easily led and anxious to please.
They couldn't seem to grasp the complexity required of them.
He even commended them for their model testimonies.
And they smiled at him. They smiled at him in the day
as they had smiled at me in the night. So I stopped all that.
I take scant notice of the proceedings now. I doze.
Or I have a bit of a shout when I feel like it.
I wander about the courtroom picking up papers. Nobody minds.
And I wait for the colour of the scents when the doors are flung open at five.
They've been green for the past few days and this impresses me.
I have the green and the cool and the mice and the fountains.
When I'm alone this weekend I shall think for a long time about them.

A White Wine for Max Ernst

A clockwork train, on the green tiled floor of a swimming pool. A loco pulling just three carriages chugs busily around in chlorinated wine. The bath is square and uniformly six feet deep. There are no tracks. The large key turns slowly in the top of the engine and never winds down. It is large enough with its butterfly wings for a child's small fingers or clumsy hands. It moves in random eights and circles. It never hits the sides of the piscine. From up here I can only taste it. The association of two or more apparently alien elements on a plane alien to both is the most potent ignition of poetry.

The X

Drunk, I spelled it with an x
as if it were an Aztec lake, or god.
These old high cultures want to get in everywhere
and don't care how they do it usually
as long as their onion cloudscapes come across,
the ones with autumn in the middle.
I'd burned my fingers earlier and now, here I was,
heating a silver shilling held in yours
to watch it blacken. There were moons
and smoking mountain pools about,
the kind of bacon atmospheres that this large month
had put on the menu right from the start,
a way of fuming paper brown
by holding it over tall glass funnels
with fire at the bottom; shallow skies
as thick and fragrant as European soups,
gazpacho andaluz for instance;
and perfect plates, in perfect restaurants.
There was a lot of the cookery book about it all
and indeed it is clear that Tuscany and Mexico
are now in the hands of a clever chef
who last night practised in your kitchen
folding tales like pancakes in the air above the stove.
The meteor storms of middle August
were busy going on outside
and being photographed,
perhaps from Perseus as well as here,
and porcupines were eating potatoes
by the side of Italian coastal highways
caring nothing for alliteration
and a tall fat man with the Baltic in his eyes
rotated a silver rouble in a candle flame
and looked out at the whitening sky
and continued to wonder what was drinking it.

The Autumn

A grainy autumn day, and all that it means to you:
street slung under the beam of the wind,
sun stranded at one end, just holding its own.
Summer's over, and perhaps we are phantoms.
The smell of the lunchtime frying is one last
dervish of brick dust, a dung-laden wind out of India.
The world is made out of sand, the people are granular.
Granular cyclists are real devils from China
and threaten to cycle right into the cinema.
I can see why the dead would want
to get back to a set-up like this.
Here comes one now. Fighting with sweet-papers,
trying to come all the way back, not making it.
A dog keeps blinking at me, and makes me want to laugh.
Grit whirls in my eyes but my glasses save me.
Poor old Brother Sun, he's seen what I'm up to.
He must get tired, just hanging around.
I watch him wipe his hand across *his* eyes.

Bard

A twelvemonth of nights,
in the press in the kitchen.
An upturned table
weighed down with old flagstones.

A twelvemonth of days,
up to here in the midden.
Necklace of redworms,
chaplet of tea-leaves.

A year of nights and days,
ludicrous, condign.
The constrained and difficult metres.

The Nail

I'm knocking a nail in.
With my heart.
The darts are on silent running.
Then they thud home.
The players call to each other.
Or rock on tables.
The music's too loud.
It involves the lungs with the sternum.
The blue-lipped male stuffs food down his throat.
I regard his opposable thumbs.
Beer left standing ebbs and flows with the moon.
There are arcane tides.
Still chambers in the hearts of gorillas
Fill with phlegm and clutter.

Gentle families cough and die on gravel-shelves.
They rinse small bitter plums.
Or else are here in this bass thump.
There are worlds of call and colour.
A stretched clock in the breast.
I'm knocking a sandwich home.
I'm knocking a nail in.
I'm hammering with my blood.

April

paranoia

yellow and green stripes
on plastic
detergent containers

faucets splashing water
round aluminium sinks

white tiles
long winded walks
cold sweats
and restaurants

daffodils

the old Dutch-style facades behind which
you, Alan,
imagine the rape of Indonesia being planned

Donegal

Two months later I make my red song,
I re-enact our waking up.
You haven't slept all night, you've been frightened,
you have said the Lord's Prayer three times.
I'm not surprised. It's the red hand of Ulster.
The wind is still high and has blown into the room
a red debris, while your Englishman slept.
Where did you find it, Ann? What does it eat?
The jokes we made before I came over inform the visit.
It does, in fact, discover its diet here
and two months later still hungers
for the fuchsia hedges that blood the back roads;
the crimson beak and white bones
of an oyster catcher, scattered behind the dunes;
the evening sun that fires the stones
of the penal altar.
It is more than memory.
The wind that carried us all through that day
and back round to the night
blows unmistakably red again.
We stand on the edge of Sessiagh
and watch the terns slicing the cold lake.
You say you will teach me the local way
to get my eyes picked out.
We climb the track to the cottage, to spend our final night.
You lie awake, while your Englishman sleeps.
I pad abroad in my guise of red fox,
biting the townland.

The Sigh

My girl, my girl.
I turn from the mantelpiece.
A cold milk carton
comforts and weights each hand.
I address you aloud to end
sitting here thinking about you.
A balletic rise and turn
is the consequent action
which will take me to the kitchen.
I've not made
this particular formal move before.
I suppose I sigh tenderly.
I'd make us both a cup of tea
if you weren't a thousand miles away from me.

A Vernacular Tale

I did some washing yesterday. I got my old washing machine out and decided to wash the red blanket. I used to be scared of the washing machine. My wife was always hinting it was dangerous to use, the same time berating me for not using it. When she left she left me the usual parting letter plus three pages of crabbed notes labelled Instructions for Operating Washing Machine. It took me a long time to pluck up the courage. Anyway, I did the blanket and lots of hairs came off. There were long brown ones, my own; long red henna'd ones, my wife's; and some long blonde hairs that belonged to an Irish girl called Ann. They all got twisted together. I should have changed the water before doing the normal weekly load, but I didn't. When I took the rest of the stuff out I realised I'd left a paper.handkerchief in one of the pockets. It got shredded up by the paddle and everything was covered in bits. I was also doing some washing for my lodger and I didn't think she'd appreciate this. Shelagh, I said, they've come out clean but you'll have to spend some time tomorrow picking these bits off your nice white blouse. Let's have a look, she said. What, you mean these short brown hairs that've collected on my collar? What? I said. Let's have a look. Oh, no, those are off the dog. We used to have this dog. It was always jumping on the bed.

Aloft

Knowing how to start is this time
knowing how slowly the sky
revolves, how slowly.

When she left you what she thieved
from you she cast into the night,
where it hangs there,
pricked out in stars.

Your pain is equalled only by
the consolation of the heavens.
The atlas greets its own
and something goes on, aloft,
that you cannot fathom.

In a million years or so
it will lengthen the Handle,
or brighten the Sword, on its Belt.
You won't be here, Peter, but maybe
you'll leap from your gravel and
swing by it, swing by it.

Cemetery

He sat in the back of the bus
and stared out at the stones

It was snowing
and there were fine dark hairs on his hand

He watched the sycamores,
pacing the round moon

Black and white he thought
as his lean shadow broke free

Black and white,
wiping the window with his sleeve

Seventh of April

Hardly frightened at all today. I found a candle in a drawer. I stood it in the centre of an earthenware dish and lit it. I felt quite calm. I thought of my life on the great globe. The candle was the kind you put on birthday cakes. The dish was about three inches in diameter and had once cost tuppence from a gardening shop. Basho went his own way right up to the end. He said that *every* poem was a death poem and he didn't need to write a special one.

The Drainage

When he got out of bed the world had changed.
It was very cold. His breath whitened the room.
Chill December clanked at the panes.
There was freezing fog.
He stepped outside.
Not into his street but a flat wet landscape.
Sluices. Ditches. Drains. Frozen mud and leafcake. Dykes.
He found he knew the names of them all.
Barber's Cut. Cold Track. Lament. Meridian Stream.
He found himself walking.
It was broad cold day but the sky was black.
Instead of the sun it was Orion there.
Seeming to pulse his meaning down.
He was naked. He had to clothe himself.
The heifers stood like statues in the fields.
They didn't moan when he sliced the hides from them.
He looked at the penknife in his hand.
The needle, the thread, the clammy strips.
Now his face mooned out through a white hole.
The cape dripped. He knew he had
the bounds of a large parish to go.
His feet refused to falter.
Birds sat still in the trees.
Fast with cold glue. Passing their clumps
he watched them rise in their species.
The individuals. Sparrow. Starling. Wren.
He brought them down with his finger.
Knife needle and thread again.
It happened with the streams.
Pike barbel roach minnow gudgeon.
Perch dace eel. Grayling lamprey bream.
His feet cracked puddles and were cut on mud, They bled.
There was movement. He pointed. He stitched.
His coat hung reeking on him.

He made cut after cut in the cold.
Coldness and the colours of blood.
Red blue and green. He glistened.
He stitched through white fat.
Weight of pelts and heads. Nodding at the hem.
Feathers. Scales. Beaks and strips of skin.
He had the bounds of a large parish to go.
Oh Christ, he moaned. Sweet Christ.
The Hunter hung stretched in the Sky.
He looked at the creatures of the bankside.
He glistened. He pointed. He stitched.

The Flowers of Finland

Taken. Under-taken. Taken.
Words from a dream...
Stop. All wrong.
Words from a reverie.
Work on in Shapeland.
Stop.
The flowers of Finland.
Right.
Like rockets. Cut it out.
Are big trees.
And the round lakes of Finland.
Maybe.
Like white ashtrays.
Right.

Anywhere will do to start.
It always has.
Language is the propensity.

We have the template,
then anything you care to mention.
A fort in Georgia called 'Kiss my Backside'
commemorates the answer to a summons to surrender.
I read a lot, jot some of it down, forget the most.
So I have to look for the notebooks.
Sometimes I read about the Balkans,
at others about America, or the Great Blasket.
Mainly it's the language interests me.
Wherever you go you find it stares out at you
from a similar nest of sticks.
And they are white ones,
and verse epistles from gifted New Yorkers
are sorely needed to elucidate why.
I think I am moving toward some kind of expressionism,
or else 'why else are we here?'

Well, there's a new house for a start, and therefore much pride.
Much pleasure in the squareness of rooms
and the smallness and depth of windows.
Pleasure in walls.

After my head hit the windscreen
I thought of Auden's words
that without a cement of blood they would not safely stand.
Then there was coming down in the dawn
and drinking orange juice from square containers.
Listening to birdsong. And feeling what used to be
called happy. Feeling nothing. Feeling that French words
do much more justice to certain concepts, if rarely,
and that squareness might be one of them.
Feeling very little really.
Knowing I was drinking pineapple juice,
knowing that the truth about the world
mightn't be the best way
of getting some things down.

Cat Nights

(for Sean O'Brien)

These are the cat nights, friend,
Like the dog days, only not so hot,
And not in Latin, either.
Latin's for the daylight, friend,
But these nights
Are taken from the Greek.
Gold might be what we order our mornings in
But on cat nights, down here that is,
Silver is what we use between ourselves.
For we are named for the moon.
A stream from her cold purse
Disanoints the day,
And darkens the terraces,
And strands the corner shops
Like blocks of pale stone
In the ruined fields of Asia.
And this is how we stand:
Grinning deviously,
Drinking our white smoke.
It is the last night in the City again,
The thrilling last before death or slavery
And here, on time, come the eponymous cats,
Flitting below the walls like laughter
So that we laugh too. The cats are on time.
The cats can be trusted, friend.
The cats will lend us their black
And brindled suits.

A Daft Place

A daft place this.
Going south from here to the river
is to follow a daft line of questioning.
First the estate with its daft new names,
then the suburbs with their daft front doors,
then the ruined Town, with its sweet daft secrets.
Everywhere here the domestic architecture
is either daft or missing.
Daft to start with, ruined by daftness, daft in being gone.
Even the river mud is dafter than we care to own.
There are more gulls on the dustbins than on the estuary now.
All gone daft. All eating daft food, like us.

In the Dakotas

He stumbles out of town again,
barefoot, as usual.
His boots are still in the saloon,
either full of beer, in mid air, or being shot at.
He wonders what happened to his shirt.
Hugging his crotch, he wonders what happened to his hat.
It's the same every Saturday.
Cowboys with their tiresome talents
recognise the dude, even in his ranch clothes,
and alter, hide, or simply steal
whatever garments he dares to come in wearing.
He dreams of joshing them, one day, by driving in naked,
but doesn't trust their humour. Better to keep buying pants.
He sees a kind of pattern to it all.
Everyone profits, except for him.
The Boss, who persists in sending him shopping each week,
despite the split sacks and the hamstrung mules,
is obviously getting a pay-off.
The niggrers and mexes, who creep out after dark,
won't mind dining on spilled beans,
and even the whores from the flop house get a free afternoon
seeing him back to the Curly K
as the obligatory fenceload of jeering broads.
He reckons he's the mainstay of their entertainment,
but what about their economy?
At night in the bunkhouse he ponders the structures
of a weird cartel he's come to postulate.
Who owns the empty livery stable?
Who the general store?
Why does the railroad swerve to arrive
in this clearly tumbleweed town?
Who are all these genteel ladies married to,
the ones who scatter before gunplay,

since all the men are unwashed oafs
who lounge on the sidewalks all day,
waiting to brawl with him?
Where does their money come from?
Slugs are seventy cents apiece
yet they all pack Colts which they shoot off like their mouths,
knocking holes like dinner plates in strangers
or spinning cans off rails.
Perhaps they trade a special kind of horse,
bred to pull bars from the back walls of gaols.
Perhaps they are mainly morons,
planted by the Feds for a political purpose,
like terrifying the Arapaho.
Sometimes it seems to him
that even the desert sun conspires
and he wonders, implausibly,
whether they are watched from the rim of the hills,
whether money changes hands,
since never was light more suited to dying in,
to scanning such daft brutalities,
or observing such ignorant townships.

In Britain

The music, on fat bellied instruments.
The fingers, swarming down ladders
into the bubbling cauldrons of sound.
The mouths, greasy, encouraging the prying fingers
with songs of fecund stomachs.
The hands, transferring to the singing mouths
whatever is lifted through the scum.
The choicest morsels, the collops of dog and the
gobbets of pig. The orchestras and bands,
the minstrelsy arranged in tiers,
dripping on each other. The larded steps.
The treacherous floors in the wooden galleries.
The garlands of offal, plopping on heads
from a height of some feet.
The offal sliding off down the front of the face,
or over the neck and ears. The offal reposing like hats.
The curly grey-white tubes, dangling jauntily
above the left eye of the bagpipe player.
The guests, similarly festooned.
The guests at their conversation,
abundance of dogs and pigs in these islands.
The guests at their serious business, lying in pools.
The stories, farting and belching across the puddled boards.
The gross imaginations, bulging with viscera.
The heads full of stories, the stories thwacked like bladders.
The stories steaming in time to the music.
The stories, chewed like lumps of gristle.
The stories describing extravagant herds.
The stories, reasons for killing each other.

In Belgium

Call it Belgium,
where the nights are always blue,
and where the dawn goes off like a gun.
Say it is a high white room in Belgium,
where the moon lights your thin face
and the face of your lover, who must be Belgian.
Know that in Belgium
all degrees and states of night are Belgian,
and morning springs like traps
around high white boxes
where Belgians wait for birdsong.
All the best jokes are told in Belgium,
in darkened bistros and downstairs rooms
to poets, by slender Belgian policemen,
paid back in verses from the Belgian floor.
When it rains in Belgium they open their umbrellas,
but only to make love beneath them,
or to imagine other Belgians doing so.

The Web

(for Douglas Dunn)

A summer noon. About to rain.
Brahms is on the Third. So is last night's pain.

Centennial terrace. Spick and span.
Literary tropes. A passing Chinaman.

Keystone, lozenge, yellow brick...
But picture windows make me sick.

Purple mascara, round the 'wind's eye'.
Lady Etymology, teach me how to cry.

'Horn of eye-paint'. Sky full of water.
Keren-happuch, Job's fair daughter.

Skirts of rain, voice of thunder.
Language and history make me tender.

A pole with wires, that serves the street,
The Web, where all our voices meet.

A Civil Garden

Microglosses for Tony Petch

1

Black tea, as at a funeral,
my girl would say you
'lived' in the kitchen

I suppose we'd say
we lived out here right now,
in the 'garden'

2

The rules are exciting:
I may not dump night-soil,
I may not boil soap,
I may not erect steam roundabouts.
Very old and exciting.

3

Or the yellow marrow: topped at noon
and then laid out on the lid of the dustbin,

when he went he took the sun,
he took his name and number with him

Two Urns

> 'Tis time to observe Occurrences, and let nothing remarkable escape us
>
> SIR THOMAS BROWNE

Long expected they arrive at last,
Maybe from the coast of Africa,
two urns that now stand breathing quietly
beneath the wall of the shed,
between the keg of earth and the water butt,
like patient animals. They come at night.
I go to my back window and can just make out
their grey flanks like elephant hide
heave down twice into a stiff low pulse,
cooling and beginning to reserve
the silver air of this specific garden.
Algeria burned, or Tunis impelled them
to come where the soft fruit-canes
would stand on the wind in salutation,
tulip and big daisy and phlox
calling to my migratory jars
to crumble into sand and reconstitute here,
where I welcome them. They stand in air
and the grass grows up around their feet
and rain collects and dries inside them.
By day they swell until they speak like drums
and at midnight I can bend my ear to them
or watch from the doorway the stars to which they call,
pulling their hard coats closer about them,
swallowing white fire,
working their round mouths on Sun and Moon
or the flight of birds, woodsmoke, silence,
the tracks of this or that slow planet.

The Library Steps

It is spring, and still cold.
The air on the library steps smells of cucumber
just like it did in the autumn.
I come straight from the lake in the park,
and its black and white geese
have kept on beating towards me.
They flew out of the Stone Age
and then turned south to the river,
which means that the river must lie behind my eyes.
We were drinking last night.
A long saloon with mirrors tilts on a cold swell
and will be going down quite soon,
taking our reflections with it.
Where will we drink next week,
when everything is altered?
The landlord died and then we forgot his death
but now his widow's 'year' is finally up, it seems.
The big bombers are also *up*, every evening now.
There are fish that live in swift and clear chalk waters
and when their flesh is broken they too smell of cucumber.

A Book

Their love is a book, then, which makes their hearts
deep and meaningful chunks of it.
Picaresque fiction, with a hundred devices,
they can't remember how it started any more,
only why it keeps them together: put *this* one down,
and you might never pick up another. You might lose
interest, even the ability. You could end up reading
poetry, or going to the library.
It all has the feel of the last twenty pages
of a book they've been reading for the last twenty years.
She alone has read more books, real ones, in this room
than the breaths he takes on an average visit.
Long ones. Short ones. Some as big as his head.
Slow ones, deep ones, ones abandoned or flung
aside somewhere, short rapid hot ones.
What wears him down is her liking for metaphor.
The chapters take months, which suggests, doesn't it,
that whatever they're reading is still in the writing?
At least it would explain the stops and starts,
the mistakes, the glaring ambiguity,
the days when they both want to read but can't get
down to it. It's possible they are writing it together,
but he rejects this as fanciful. It's not their own waste-
paper bins they kneel around on bad days,
desperate for a read. There isn't even a way of knowing
when there'll be a few more pages ready.
It wouldn't be so bad if they agreed upon the text
but each relates incidents, with relish sometimes,
that the other won't admit to. 'Blood' as a motif
she scorns to notice, but the scene in the café is precious.
He liked the bit where it rained all month
but she points out that it must have been blood.

Venery

The king is out hunting, and here is his lodge.
It is high hot noon, as every thing declares.
Four black bees drone about the threshold, while the mountain
hangs gold and blue a long way back.
The hard matt meadow stretches green right down
to the endless wood. Discs of bright brown clay
shew in the grass like coins, and there are white flowers.
A leathern bottle swells on its back in the shavings under the wall.
Dropped at dawn the sun is on it now
and I hear its contents quicken. The day stays at noon.
The birds are still, but the bees keep on droning.
A moment's breadth of air slaps the splintered hall.
An inch of white daub soundlessly flakes and falls.
Forty yards away, between the house and the forest,
a solitary cedar post the height of a man
leans at a slight angle. The sun catches its sides,
where they've been planed. The grass at the foot is lush
and chimes with dry voices that fill the pasture.
Back the other way, behind the house,
the kitchen garden looks uphill to the haze.
It is quite extensive, and the beans are in flower.
Blue light flows down off the rocks and makes everything white.
A door stands open. The square dark holes of the windows
mirror the caves up the mountain.
The man and his wife, the old retainers,
move in the dark recesses of the rooms.
Their actions are inexplicable. They seem to believe
they are somewhere else. The dog looks at them.
A dozen miles away the king washes his knife
in the stream that came by here this morning.
The sons and daughters of the dog give tongue delightedly.
The huntsmen throw handballs of bread and blood to them.

The Residents, 1840

(for Douglas Houston)

1 *Menzies at Mosul*

The mud-walled cities. I approve of them.
Law and commerce and scholarship.
Monday to Thursday I nip dried fruits
between my finger and my thumb,
I walk in the nerveless gardens.
Friday to Sunday I stand in front of monoliths,
I cross the square where hands are cut off.
I am Musulman, Christian, Jew.
Three days of Sabbath end to end
delight me as they would my father,
therefore I keep all of them.
I further my inquiry into the cuneus, or wedge.
I correspond with Farquhar, a long way east,
about the coathanger scripts of India,
but only because I have to.
I share his delight in perfect styli
but not in his employment of them.
He sits there painted blue
and writes he believes he is Krishna.

2 *Farquhar in Bengal*

The waterways here. I love their teeming life.
Fishes and temples and spices in sacks.
In the mornings I do what I have to,
the rest of the time I think about myself.
I have given up learning for the necklace of sense
which my woman brings me in the evening.
She plays her narrow flute.
She anoints my glistening back.
I don't believe in anything any more.
How could I, when everything is true?
I have seen the demonic tree the Brahmin climbed,
determined to find the branches empty.
He threw himself joyfully down.
I have listened to the chakora bird,
which subsists entirely upon moonbeams.
I shan't be replying to Menzies' last.
He knows all I knew now
and begins to believe he is God.

A Riddle

> Close to death, and heedless of the State, the Emperor Justinian sits far into the night. In the company of a few old priests he is pondering the macabre riddles of the Divine Will. In another place, a navigator is slowly bleeding to death in the back of a doomed bomber.

Justinian. My eighty-somethingth year. I get mixed up.
Navigating, I think. Darkness crumping into insurrections,
or flak. Light reduced to what will serve a table.
Light remaining the problem. When the moon
shines through the palace windows, it breaks upon the floor.
They catch the moon in metal bowls, and use it to finger us out.
What am I doing here, forty years on? Or is it longer?
The red and white of the maps recall the gift
my stooping priests bestow upon the people.
Their hands reach forward. They sit frozen in their gear.
The world lies done in coloured cubes upon the palace floor.
A flickering candle. Dropping through cloud over Aachen
it was Anastasis, as bright as day. And I was Christ,
and I reached for the hand of Adam. Never grasping.
How can this remorseless bird be flying so high up?
What life obtains inside the Dove? Where is the dawn?
This night must either be ending now, or going on for ever.
It is one more riddle. I plot and plot, but cannot get us home.

Roses

Roses are coloured holes in the evening.
When the light fails birds fly into them.
They wriggle through into open caves
and perch on steps and ledges.
They make honest articulate parliaments.
They administer themselves until morning.

Clues

twittering, failed to script
soliloquies
for night long watch

filled with dread
made a queue

now Friendly Isles rescind
an oared craft,
and put into words
unhappily
face covers like tough old beans

Saying Goodbye

The problem is how to address yourself.
Do you call yourself you, or do you use your Christian name?
It's hard to know. The first is gamey, dandified, coy.
Whatever adjective you care to use to say that something isn't so.
The second would be better if you could spell it Xtian,
starting with an X, the kind of happy shorthand a pietist might use.
It would also be better if you didn't already hate it more
than anything else in the world, the way young girls do.
It would be better never to have begun,
because how to call you over to yourself prevents you getting on
to what you thought you had in mind, which was to tell yourself
to give it up, to go and live in Tunis, go and live in the sun.
But who doesn't tell themselves that? Madmen. *Vicious* people.
Fools. You wanted to say how brutally you aspect yourself
to all that makes you you, that you know it, and look! look!
it's going to be different this time. This time there isn't
any kidding going on. You'll give up reading history. You'll give up
writing about the moon. You'll really forgive yourself this time.
And just for a moment it really seems you will.
You remember all the rhetoric, and all the metrical helps,
and you actually feel proud that you're going to say goodbye.
Goodbye, 'Perhaps' (old friend!) Goodbye, 'As if' – you really
held out promise for a while. Goodbye, all the lapidary reticence
which postured under the stars, as if you'd really gone mad
and come out on the other side, where pain is henceforth dignified
by standing in a winter arboretum, and not just going out and getting drunk,
which of course you did as well. Goodbye, goodbye, a drawn out death.
The goodbyes fall thick and fast, as if you really meant it
and would go away a sadder and a wiser man, not even caring
to deny yourself those clichés, which is what you were taught to do,
indeed what you now teach to others. The trouble with language, here and now,
is that it's riddled with devices, far more tropes than we ever
teach our children, more ways of saying nothing than anything else.

Even goodbyes habitually use the selfsame wings, for flying on,
as are flapped by young hulloes, so you can't exactly use them
to tell yourself off with, not without enjoying it,
not without the grave suspicion that everything's going wrong again.
Do what you like, but you still feel that awful interest in the
joining-words, all the bits you tack together with, to make good sentences.
You promise yourself to write bad sentences,
but *real* bad sentences, and I'm sorry about this, are *really* 'good',
and the others just embarrass you. There's no escape.
Despise the grown-up children, with their grown-up talk,
there isn't any escape. Mention linguistic events, you'll go
blue in the face. Talk about simply using the medium,
seeing what it will do like a painter does. You'll just go blue.
All the time you know you're as liable to go blue as they are,
all the time you know there's nowhere left to go
unless you abandon it altogether, which is what you always decide.
Except you backslide frequently. You give up English English
to go for strolls in refined American parks, just long enough
to hate them all for being so damnably insolent. You tell your friend
that you and your other friend disagree about the language,
but really you just hate each other, and would be better off with knives.
At least most knives don't open their extremely thin lips and tell you
their misanthropy is equalled only by their love of children. Even if it's true.

NOTES

That Way Inclined (227): Paul Klee was in Tunisia in 1914. I had in mind such paintings as 'Flagged Town'.

Building the Titanic (233): The 'Grecian Urn' syndrome. These workers are fixed as irrevocably, in a well-known contemporary photograph, as Keats's 'marble men and maidens overwrought' on the sides of the urn. A 'Cold Industrial'.

Geography (233): The poem was compiled from scattered sentences in M.H. Law's *How to Read German*. For example, 'Schadenfreude ist eine sehr beliebte Freude, aber sie ist nie böse gemeint.' Amused and chilled, I was led to uncover this underlying structure of a sentimental, High European geography.

Strange Ubiquitous History (236): A visual expression of this dynamic of trees can be found in the photograph by Fay Godwin on page 131 of *Worlds: Seven Modern Poets*, ed. Geoffrey Summerfield (Penguin, 1974).

Bard (244): Training in the old Bardic schools of Ireland was long and rigorous. The austerities here are "domestic" variants of some of the ascetic disciplines involved.

Donegal (246): The Red Hand is the heraldic badge of Ulster. Sessiagh is pronounced 'Shesher' to rhyme, more or less, with 'thresher'. Under the anti-Catholic Penal Laws of the eighteenth century only a certain number of 'registered' priests was tolerated. Unregistered priests, who were liable to be hanged, drawn and quartered if apprehended, celebrated Mass clandestinely at '*penal altars*' – in this case, a rock in a field. The whole system of apartheid embodied in these statues was described by Edmund Burke as 'a machine of as wise and elaborate contrivance for the impoverishment and degradation of the people, and the debasement in them of human nature itself, as ever proceeded from the perverted ingenuity of man'.

Cat Nights (254): *'Disanoint'* is a lovely verb that I came across in Keats: 'for Fate / Had pour'd a mortal oil upon his head, / A disanointing poison'. *Hyperion*, II. 96-8.

The Web (260): 'Window' is derived from the Old Norse *vindauga* – 'wind-eye'. *Keren-happuch* was the last of the children born to Job after God began to prosper him again. The name means 'horn of eye-paint' and, in English, is pronounced with the stress on the first and third syllables. See Job 42. 14.

The Residents, 1840 (266): The Tree of Death stood in the precincts of a temple at Prayāga. The story is told in chapter 6 of *The Land of the Great Image* by Maurice Collis (Faber, 1943). Letters in the various North Indian scripts which derive from Nāgarī consist of vertical and 'distinctive' strokes which depend from a horizontal line. Hence 'coathanger'.

A Riddle (268): *Anastasis* is Christ's Harrowing of Hell. I was imagining a moment of timelessness at the moment of death in which these individual souls meet and are confused. The poem shews the effects of reading Randall Jarrell concurrently with H. St L.B. Moss's *The Birth of the Middle Ages*, from which part of the epigraph is adapted.

Clues (269): This poem was compiled, with slight alterations, from consecutive clues in a crossword puzzle. I was fascinated by the fraught and interrupted Odyssey it seemed to hint at. Unable now to remember the source, I hope that the original compiler, should he recognise his own hand, will forgive my borrowing.

INDEX OF TITLES & FIRST LINES

Index of titles and first lines

(Titles are shown in italics, first lines in roman type.)

EU DECLARATION OF GPSR CONFORMITY

Books published by Bloodaxe Books are identified by the EAN/ISBN printed above our address on the copyright page and manufactured by Lightning Source at the printing works indicated in their code. This declaration of conformity is issued under the sole responsibility of the publisher, the object of declaration being each individual book produced in conformity with the relevant EU harmonisation legislation with no known hazards or warnings, and is made on behalf of Bloodaxe Books Ltd on 10 April 2026 by Neil Astley, Managing Director, editor@bloodaxebooks.com.